202

THE WAR
IN THE
MEDITERRANEAN
1940–1943

THE WAR
IN THE
MEDITERRANEAN
1940–1943

Bernard Ireland

LEO COOPER

First published in 1993 by Arms & Armour Press
Reprinted in 2004 by
LEO COOPER
an imprint of Pen & Sword Books Limited
47 Church Street
Barnsley
South Yorkshire
S70 2AS

A CIP catalogue record for this book is available from
the British Library

ISBN 1-84415-047-X

Cartography by Peter Burton

Printed in England by
CPI UK

Contents

TWO

'Parallel War'

June to September 1940

THREE DAYS before Mussolini made his fateful declaration from the balcony of the Palazzo Venezia, *Supermarina* ordered all Italian-flag merchant shipping into Axis-controlled or neutral ports. The instruction was hopelessly late. Of a fleet of 786 ships, grossing over 3.3 million tons, about one-third (212, of 1.2 million tons) were marooned in foreign ports. Few among the Italian leadership realized that, without a shot being fired, the country had suffered a disaster of the first order.

Mussolini's immediate problem was to get into the war before it was all over. A beleaguered, post-Dunkirk Britain looked likely to sue for peace in order to avoid invasion. French military thinking appeared ossified, incapable of reacting to fluid, mechanized warfare with sufficient speed. Just twelve days after the last troops were lifted from Dunkirk's equipment-strewn beaches, Paris fell.

On 28 March France and the United Kingdom had declared that neither would conclude or negotiate an armistice or peace treaty except by mutual agreement. The day before Paris fell, 13 June, the French Premier, Paul Reynaud, advised Prime Minister Churchill that an armistice needed to be considered. President Roosevelt could offer equipment but was otherwise powerless to intervene and, on 16 June, the British agreed to the French proposal but excluded themselves from involvement as they had announced their intention of continuing the struggle. Consent for a separate French peace was given, 'provided, but only provided' that the French Fleet sailed to British-controlled harbours, pending a decision on its future. For the previous ten days, the British War Cabinet had been concerned about this particular matter. With Italy and Germany in active combination and Japan's involvement increasingly likely, the loss of French support was serious enough to see its Fleet acquired by the Axis was to contemplate disaster.

Admiral Darlan, the French C-in-C, stated unequivocally that to hand over the Fleet to the enemy would be counter to tradition and honour; if faced with an impossible situation, it would be scuttled. The British view was tempered by practicality: as long as the ships existed, Germany could always exert pressure—for example, threaten to destroy Paris—to enforce their handover. Old rivalries surfaced, with Darlan reportedly commenting that he 'did not create a fleet in order to offer it to the British'. As a compromise, some of the major units were sailed to French colonial ports.

The Franco-German armistice was signed on 22 June 1940. A clause stipulated the assembly and disarming of the Fleet at specified ports in return for a 'solemn declaration' by the Germans that they would claim no part of it. This apparently generous gesture was effectively an admission that any attempt to impose demands would only have prompted a mass exodus to British ports. Inactivity was the preferred option. Two days later the French concluded a separate armistice with the Italians. The *Duce* demanded no less than the surrender of the French Navy and Air Force, together with the handover of Corsica, Savoy, Nice and part of Tunisia. Hitler, however, wished to treat the French leniently for the moment and had Mussolini withdraw his demands—which he did with great reluctance.

From 25 June, the date on which the armistice took effect, those French warships not already on their way to join the British were confined to their home ports, their ensigns half-masted. Darlan signalled that France had gained generous armistice terms and would be only partially occupied. This agreement would not be jeopardized, and all conditions would be strictly observed and appeals from 'former allies' ignored: 'Let us think as Frenchmen; let us act as Frenchmen'. Other than those at Toulon and those under British control, French units were at Algiers (four heavy and three light cruisers), at Martinique (two light cruisers and the aircraft carrier) and at Dakar and Casablanca (one battleship at each); at Mers-el-Kebir the usual presence had been reinforced by the Atlantic Squadron and moored there were the two fast *Dunkerque*s, two older battleships and six 'super-destroyers'. It was the pair of *Dunkerque*s and the two *Richelieu*s in particular that the British Government could not allow to pass into enemy hands.

Admiral Darlan was no great anglophile and he ignored Churchill's extravagantly worded appeals to rally the Allied cause. While the British never doubted the honour of Darlan's motives and intentions, there was still the high probability of German duplicity. The ships had to be put beyond the enemy's reach. The French Navy was in an ambivalent position. During nine months of ocean warfare it had co-operated and strengthened its ties with the Royal Navy, but it was now scattered. Most personnel wished to remain loyal to France's legitimate government but, with the nation in a divided and confused state, it was difficult to determine what constituted legitimacy.

Even without the French units being appropriated by the Axis, the Royal Navy in the Mediterranean had seen its position change from one of a shared and comfortable majority to one of being considerably outnumbered. Since the end of the Norwegian campaign Cunningham's fleet had grown steadily, to four battleships, one carrier, seven cruisers, 22 destroyers and a dozen submarines. These were, however, confined effectively to the eastern basin, based at the inadequate Alexandria.

With French facilities no longer available, Malta now appeared indispensable. As the island was assumed to be untenable in the face of Italian air attack, Churchill briefly considered abandoning the eastern basin and concentrating on the excellent base facilities at Gibraltar. Convinced, nonetheless, that the Italians' quantity outmatched their quality, the Premier decided to take a gamble. On 28 June 1940, therefore, a separate striking force was established at Gibraltar. Known as Force 'H', and operating under the flag of Vice-Admiral Sir James Somerville in the battlecruiser *Hood*, the group included the battleships *Valiant* and *Resolution*, the carrier *Ark Royal*, a light cruiser and four destroyers. Strategically based, Somerville could operate in either the Atlantic or the Mediterranean.

Whether stationed at Alexandria or Gibraltar, Royal Navy units were too distant easily to influence either events in Malta or on the Italian sea routes to North Africa. At a time when Britain faced her greatest threat from invasion, therefore, the decision was made to reinforce substantially both the island and Egypt. A measure of the urgency felt was the decision to send the resultant convoys through the Mediterranean—previously considered to be out of the question—rather than round the Cape. The British could not know that the withdrawal of the French had altered Italian naval policy not one jot.

Within six hours of the Italian declaration of war, 35 bombers escorted by eighteen fighters began Malta's long ordeal with an attack on Valletta and its docks, and Hal Far airfield. This raid was unopposed, but a repeat performance that afternoon was met by two Gloster Sea Gladiators. These made up half the island's fighter defences and existed only because they had been 'found' broken down in crates and awaiting the carrier *Glorious*, which had been sunk off Norway. One of the quartet was quickly written off, but the remainder achieved immortality as *Faith*, *Hope* and *Charity*, holding the ring until the arrival of more modern fighters (the initial total absence of which was scandalous).

Priorities conflicted in every direction, and Malta gained four Hurricane Mk Is at the end of June only at the expense of Alexandria's defences. At home the Battle of Britain still raged, and only at the end of August could the old carrier *Argus* ferry in another dozen aircraft. This operation, 'Hurry', was the first of many such trips. It was, however, fortunate that the Italians, once seriously challenged, could be persuaded easily to jettison their bomb loads or fly at far greater altitudes.

Churchill instructed that further warship movements were to be utilized for the building up of the island's military strength. Personnel were to be drawn from what he disparagingly referred to as 'police duties'. Only with sufficient strength to resist an invasion by a 'twenty or thirty thousand-man' Italian expeditionary force, adequate anti-aircraft defences and fighter aircraft could Malta be felt secure enough to act again as a fleet base.

The deepest concern about the possible fate of the French Fleet led to the inevitable tragedy on 3 July 1940. At Alexandria, Admiral Cunning-ham had succeeded in persuading the French to demilitarize peacefully. In British ports, many French vessels were boarded and secured by force—an unpalatable but often necessary course of action that enabled the Prime Minister to point out how easy it would be for the Germans to do the same. The powerful squadron at Mers-el-Kebir particularly occupied the minds in the British War Cabinet. A force of uncertain loyalties, it was placed strategically on the flank of a major area of operations.

As part of Operation 'Catapult', the overall actions covering the French Fleet, Admiral Somerville was directed to take Force 'H' to Oran and present a hastily drafted ultimatum. Its preamble stressed Britain's continuing respect for and friendship with France but emphasized her resolve to remove the warships beyond German reach. Four options were tabled: fight alongside the British against a common foe; sail, with reduced crews, to a British port; sail, with reduced crews and under British escort, to a French West Indies port and there be demilitarized to British satisfaction; or scuttle the ships within six hours.

In the event, the French refused all these choices, and Somerville was ordered to employ any necessary force to achieve the main aim. With rare compassion, the Admiralty recognized that Somerville was being charged with 'one of the most disagreeable and difficult tasks' but directed him to carry it through 'relentlessly'. Early on 3 July, therefore, Somerville arrived off Oran with his three 15in capital ships, *Ark Royal,* two cruisers and eleven destroyers. One of the latter, HMS *Foxhound*, entered the French base carrying Captain Holland, commander of *Ark Royal* and, as recent Naval Attaché in Paris, well known to the French. He awaited Admiral Gensoul for hours, the Frenchman refusing to associate himself with anything smacking of an ultimatum. The first three options would break the terms of the Franco-German armistice and attract the direst repercussions. Pride ruled out scuttling. The British could either accept French assurances or be prepared to fight. In a critical misjudgement, aircraft from *Ark Royal* dropped mines in the approaches to the base while negotiations were still in hand. This action served only to stiffen French resolve.

Somerville extended the deadline to allow Gensoul to exchange signals with Darlan in France. While the latter was already immersed in the problems of moving the French Admiralty to Vichy, the former inexplicably failed to point out the full range of options given him. The situation was ripe for miscalculation. When, at 1500, Gensoul finally met Holland, it was to tell him that he had been instructed to meet force with force.

Somerville, waiting outside, was becoming edgy. He was vulnerable to submarine attack, and increasingly blunt signals from the Admiralty warned of French reinforcements. Finally, he was instructed explicitly that the French must comply with the terms, scuttle themselves or 'be sunk by you before dark'. At 1612 he signalled that, if the ultimatum were not met, he would commence firing at 1630. Although the French had raised steam, they remained 'Mediterranean-moored', stern-on to the mole, with anchors down. In close proximity to each other, they were in a poor position to fight yet offered a compact target.

Eventually, at 1656, the British capital ships opened fire at 15,000yds (13,700m) with aircraft spotting. The veteran *Provence* responded immediately, firing across *Dunkerque*, laying to her starboard. As he had stated, Gensoul had not fired first, but he now found himself at a terrible disadvantage as his four capital ships tried to slip and manoeuvre into the fairway.

Strasbourg was first away, and her just-vacated berth was promptly hit by a full 15in British salvo. By 1710 she was making 15kts towards the open sea, but, even as her sister, *Dunkerque*, got under way, she was heavily struck. A single 15in shell was followed immediately by a close group of three, one of which punched a hole through the roof of 'B' turret. The ship lost power, ceased fire and re-anchored, still within the confines of the harbour.

Waiting for *Dunkerque* to clear, *Provence* took several hits at 1703: ablaze and flooding rapidly, she had to be beached. Her elderly sister *Bretagne* was smothered in hits. An explosion aft caused uncontrollable fires over much of her length and, at 1709, she suddenly capsized in shallow water. Nearly one thousand of her crew were killed.

A dreadful pall of smoke obscured much of the port area, punctuated with remorseless regularity by the mast-high columns of mud-tinged water from the British salvos. Of the four large destroyers present, only one, *Mogador*, was damaged. A heavy-calibre projectile detonated her depth charge outfit, blowing off her stern. She, too, came to anchor, ablaze but with her bulkhead holding. Following thirty-six 15in salvos, Somerville checked fire at 1712. Deeply unhappy with what he had been obliged to do, the British admiral made little attempt to intercept *Strasbourg*, which, with the remaining three destroyers, made good her escape to Toulon. Here she was joined by the cruiser squadron from Algiers. French radio claimed that the damage to *Dunkerque* was of little consequence, so Somerville mounted a follow-up air strike from *Ark Royal* three days later. A torpedo exploded against a smaller ship lying alongside the battleship and, again, a full outfit of depth charges detonated, causing *Dunkerque* severe damage.

In all, this unhappy episode cost 1,297 French lives. A service previously divided in its loyalties was now united in fierce condemnation of what it perceived as British treachery. Aware of the historical precedent at Copenhagen in 1801, Prime Minister Churchill had seen the greater part of the French squadron put beyond the enemy's reach. 'The British War Cabinet,' he announced for the benefit of world opinion, 'feared nothing and would stop at nothing . . . [even at] striking ruthlessly at her dearest friends of yesterday.' Controversy will long rage over the Mers-el-Kebir affair, but the knowledge of hindsight should be tempered with an understanding of Britain's plight as she faced two dictatorships alone. The French capital ships under Axis colours constituted a potential threat which could not be allowed to develop.

Realizing the deep unpopularity of the British following their action, Hitler decided to continue to take a soft line with France in order to convince the British of the futility of their situation. Mussolini was made to abandon most of his remaining unsatisfied demands as co-victor. In particular, he was not allowed to base ships in French colonial ports. This put him at a grave disadvantage: from bases such as Bizerta, the Italian Navy could have effectively closed the Central Narrows of the Mediterranean, severely affecting British freedom of movement. While the German High Command appeared to have little appreciation of the significance of its policy of no interference in the French territories, the policy also did not appear over-important to the Italians, who still anticipated that the war would be over within weeks. The very existence of the bulk of the French Fleet at Toulon stayed the enemy's hand. This port lay in unoccupied southern France but, although the zone was under German control, there was obviously little way of preventing a mass movement of ships to Allied ports if the Axis were to break the terms of the armistice.

The failure of the Axis to exact maximum advantage from French North Africa was to be compounded by the lack of a real commitment to neutralize Gibraltar. This would not only have excluded the British from the western Mediterranean but would also have freed the Italian Navy's hand for the desired occupation of the Atlantic island groups. Germany's Operation 'Felix' would have required the full support—though not the military co-operation—of Franco's Spain. The *Caudillo*, however, was genuinely fearful of participation in further conflict and, like Mussolini before him, employed delaying tactics through demands for war *matériel* and by promoting the idea that the Suez Canal was more important than Gibraltar. In the latter he had important fellow-thinkers, not least Admiral Raeder, Supreme Commander of the German Navy. Hitler's failure to force access through Spain in order to take Gibraltar is on a par with his attitude towards the French colonies. To him, the Mediterranean was of only peripheral interest: he was more concerned with Greece and the Soviet Union, plans for action against which were well advanced. Franco was thus able to hedge until the Germans lost interest.

With the question of the French Fleet settled for the moment, the British faced two problems, namely the revitalizing of Malta and the need to establish an ascendency over the Italian Fleet. This force posed a direct invasion threat to the island, inhibited the free use of the Mediterranean and provided the means whereby Axis armies in North Africa were supported.

Mussolini's declared policy was now one of 'parallel war', defined ambiguously as 'with Germany, not for Germany, but only for Italy'. This seemed to satisfy him and, for the moment, he did little. *Supermarina* had been planning the seizure of Malta since 1938 but remained overruled by the Supreme Command: it would be a short war and, in any case, the *Regia Aeronautica* would render the island untenable. The Italian naval report, nevertheless, was quite specific: the island's occupation was the 'indispensable condition for any important Italian operations in North Africa, since just neutralizing the island . . . would not accomplish the purpose'.

Italy's approach to the likely problems of supplying forces in Libya varied between the totally pessimistic and the totally naïve. Admiral Cavagnari had written in April 1940 that such a commitment may find 'Italy [arriving] at the peace table not only with no territorial assets but also without a fleet and, perhaps, without an air force'. By June, on the other hand, the Combined Chiefs of Staff calculated that their army in North Africa could be supported adequately by a combination of civil aircraft (30 men per load), half a dozen submarines (60 to 100 tons per trip) and small merchantmen on the shortest sea route from Sicily.

Like the British, the Italians had overestimated their difficulties. Of the 500 ships left to them by virtue of their poor anticipation, only about 200 were thought suitable for the Libyan run, together with fifteen German merchantmen which hostilities had overtaken in Italian ports. After a fortnight at war, during which time nothing of note had occurred, the Italians began to think more ambitiously. On 25 June the passenger liners *Esperia* and *Victoria* left Naples on the two-day passage to Tripoli. Escorted but unmolested, they delivered a few hundred personnel and several thousand tons of supplies. They represented the first of 896 convoys which would eventually be run in support of Italian interests in North Africa.

While the convoy showed a quantitative boost, however, it highlighted a logistics problem: Tripoli was far from the front. Tobruk would be a far better choice of port, but its proximity to the British area of interest would make it hazardous for merchantmen. To test the route, therefore, the Italians decided to ferry an artillery unit across in three destroyers (*Espero*, *Ostro* and *Zeffiro*) and two torpedo boats (*Rosolino Pilo* and *Giuseppe Missori*). Sailing from Taranto, they were spotted by a Malta-based flying boat on 28 June when some fifty miles west of Zante. Vice-Admiral Tovey's 7th Cruiser Squadron was west of Crete, providing distant convoy cover, and, acting on aircraft sightings, intercepted the Italians at 1830. Hampered by their deck cargoes, the latter were unable to mount a torpedo attack but, not aware of this, Tovey opened fire from 18,000yds.

Although the Italians made little attempt to take avoiding action, the British did not score until the fifteenth salvo, which hit the leader, *Espero*. Repeating a mistake made a quarter of a century before at the Dogger Bank, the British then concentrated on the injured vessel, sinking her but allowing the remainder to escape to Benghazi. Their enormous expenditure of 6in shells caused a general British shortage of this type of ammunition for some time to come, but the Italians were quick to note the advantages of good co-operation between naval striking forces and the long-range Sunderlands of the Royal Air Force.

The Italians moved on to Tobruk where, on 5 July, they were attacked by nine FAA torpedo-carrying Swordfish operating from Sidi Barrani. Royal Air Force fighters suppressed opposition from a nearby Italian airfield, allowing the Swordfish to concentrate on their runs. *Zeffiro* was destroyed and her sister *Euro* heavily damaged; in addition, the 15,000-ton liner *Liguria* and two freighters were hit, the 3,955grt *Manzoni* ending up on her beam ends. Again, success resulted from good inter-service co-operation.

Just a week earlier at Tobruk, Marshal Balbo, Governor of Libya and theatre commander, had been killed when his aircraft was downed by 'friendly' fire. What Balbo had in rhetoric his successor, Graziani, had in caution, being very reluctant to commence the land campaign being urged upon him by Mussolini.

Italy's impressive submarine force had a poor opening month. During the space of just fifteen days in June 1940, ten boats were lost. Of these, seven fell to attack by surface ship or submarine, two were sunk by aircraft and one was lost in an accident. In the course of neutralizing the Italian naval presence in the Red Sea, the Royal Navy found the submarine *Evangelista Torricelli* on the surface near Perim Island. She was sighted by the sloop HMS *Shoreham*, which brought up three 'K' class destroyers. Unable to dive on account of unspecified damage, the Italian elected to fight it out on the surface with her single 100mm gun. Before she was destroyed she hit *Shoreham* and may have caused the torpedo explosion aboard *Khartoum*, the resultant fire from which sank the destroyer in shallow water off Perim. The British gunnery was again sub-standard, eighteen 4.7in guns taking about 35 minutes to dispose of the Italian vessel.

On 12 June *Bagnolini* had torpedoed and sunk the British cruiser *Calypso* south of Crete, but it was an isolated success. The submarines' poor basic design was ill-suited to tropical conditions, heatstroke and chlorine gas poisoning being all too common among the crews. The latter was cited as a reason for the capture of *Galileo Galilei* by the British trawler Moonstone on 19 June. Based, like *Torricelli*, at Massawa in Eritrea, *Galilei* had sunk the Norwegian tanker *James Stove* near Aden on the 16th. A two-day hunt by British anti-submarine forces had met with no success and these withdrew, leaving *Moonstone* to watch. The Italian took the bait, surfacing to finish the trawler with her two 100mm guns. The 615-ton *Moonstone* fought back, her single 4in weapon scoring two hits, killing the Italian skipper and enforcing the boat's surrender. Valuable documentation was recovered, the quickest result of which was the sinking of the submarine *Luigi Galvani*, by HMS *Falmouth* in the Gulf of Oman on 22 June. *Galilei*'s final service was to act as a stationary generating plant at Port Said.

The British, too, were saddled with submarines of inappropriate design, the big minelayers and the 'O', 'P' and 'R' classes having been built for service in the Far East. Too large, unwieldy and slow-diving, three of them (*Grampus*, *Odin* and *Orpheus*) went missing within three days in June. Always reluctant to acknowledge the effectiveness of Italian anti-submarine measures, the Admiralty ascribed the losses to mines, but all three had been sunk by surface vessels.

As part of the re-establishment of Malta as a major base, it was decided to reduce the number of non-combatant servicemen and dependents on the island. These were to be removed in two small convoys. Admiral Cunningham was to interpose the Mediterranean Fleet between them and the likely direction of approach by Italian surface forces; simultaneously, Force 'H' would create a diversion by raiding Cagliari in Sardinia. By chance, a five-ship Italian convoy left Naples on 6 July, bound for Benghazi. It was lightly supported by two 6in cruisers and destroyers but, when *Supermarina* detected British activity at Malta, two battleships and two divisions of cruisers were added. Three further cruiser divisions were placed between the convoy and Malta. Neither side realized that the other was running a convoy, and each suspected an attack on its own.

Cunningham left Alexandria late on 7 July. In the van were Tovey's five light cruisers, followed at a distance by the flagship (*Warspite*) and five destroyers. Bringing up the rear was a slow group comprising the battleships *Malaya* and *Royal Sovereign*, the carrier *Eagle* and ten more destroyers. Their position was reported that night by an Italian submarine. Then, early on the 8th, the British boat *Phoenix* sighted the enemy main body, reporting it as mid-way between Italy and Benghazi, course south. This convoy safely reached North Africa later in the day with a reported 2,200 troops, 300 armoured vehicles and 16,000 tons of supplies. Having seen their charges safely delivered, the Italian covering force turned eastwards at 1500 to meet the British.

The latter were headed roughly north-westwards and, being about mid-way between the Dodecanese and Libya, were persistently bombed from both. Italian high-level bombing had a routinely bad press, but Cunningham, in a good position to know, held it in high regard. While neither *Eagle*'s aircraft nor the fleet's guns could account for any Italian aircraft, the cruiser *Gloucester* was hit on her bridge. Among the eighteen dead was her captain. Malta-based reconnaissance aircraft now had the enemy under continuous observation, and the British convoys' sailing was delayed as the C-in-C steered for Taranto to get astride the Italians' homeward route. Decoded British radio signals led the Italians to expect Cunningham off the Calabrian coast at noon on the 9th.

At 0730 on the 9th, the enemy main body was reported only fifty miles from Cape Spartivento, the 'toe' of Italy, handy for the sanctuary of the Messina Strait. Cunningham, with an injured cruiser and four others down to fifty per cent ammunition, faced six 8in and eight 6in cruisers, and his speed was limited by the 21½kts of *Royal Sovereign*. He had three capital ships to two, but, except for *Warspite*, these were easily out-ranged by the Italian battleships, which also held a 2kt speed advantage and were under an umbrella of friendly aircraft. Cunningham related later how the situation developed like an exercise at the Portsmouth Tactical School. He was heading into a north-westerly breeze, with a slight sea and cloud-dappled sky. Each of the three elements of his force was separated by eight miles from its neighbour.

Nine torpedo-armed Swordfish from *Eagle* attacked the Italians at 1330, but, lacking experience against fast-moving targets in the open sea, their pilots enjoyed no success. Estimating that he was now between his opponent and Taranto, the C-in-C turned westwards at 1415 to close the range more rapidly. Visibility varied between 15 and 20 miles, and Tovey's cruisers, straining ahead, were ten miles in advance of Cunningham when they sighted smoke on the horizon. This proved to emanate from four heavy cruisers which, at 1514, opened proceedings at the uncomfortable range of 25,000m (27,340yds). The 6in guns of the

British light cruisers were totally out-ranged and Tovey was soon hard-pressed. With *Neptune* damaged, he fell back on to the flagship for support. *Warspite* obliged at 1526, opening fire at 26,400yds (the limit of visibility) and forcing the enemy division to turn away under cover of smoke.

Malaya succeeded in catching up, and both battleships potted at the Italians as visibility permitted. At 1550 the balance changed again as the two Italian capital ships, *Giulio Cesare* and *Conte di Cavour*, hove into sight. Despite their smaller-calibre 32cm (12.6in) batteries, they were able to straddle the British from the outset. Only *Warspite*, with her modernized mountings, could reply. Cunningham nonetheless reported his ship's practice as 'consistently good'.

At 1559 *Cesare* took a 15in hit, reducing her speed temporarily to only 18kts. Admiral Campioni took no chances, ordered smoke and altered course for the nearby Messina Strait. Lacking the speed to intercept, Cunningham remained in the area for some hours. With the Calabrian mountains clearly in view, he was subjected to protracted high-level bombing, which he described as 'most frightening'. At 1925, with nothing left to achieve, he turned for Malta. As they passed, *Eagle*'s aircraft struck at Augusta, sinking a destroyer and a tanker—a score superior to that just achieved by two battle squadrons bent on each other's destruction.

The British convoys and, eventually, the Mediterranean Fleet made Alexandria without further damage, despite continuous bombing. Both fleets had achieved their operational aim in the safe and timely arrival of their respective convoys, but Campioni, making history as the first Italian to join battle with the Royal Navy, had yielded too easily.

Admiral Cunningham, for his part, was dismayed by the inadequacies of his major units, the 25-year old armament of which was out-ranged not only by the guns of the enemy's smaller battleships but also by those of his 8in cruisers. Coupled with an edge in speed, the Italians were in a position to dictate the course of an action. Dismissing the *Royal Sovereign*s as 'a constant anxiety', he requested two or three more modernized *Queen Elizabeth*s, which also mounted a useful high-angle (H/A) secondary armament. The elderly *Eagle* had been severely shaken by the Italian bombing, having been near-missed on several occasions. Over two thousand 100kg and 250kg bombs had been dropped, any one of which could have penetrated her deeply before exploding. One of the new armoured-deck carriers was, therefore, requested, as were heavy cruisers, of which the Royal Navy had few. Amazingly, Tovey's smaller ships had hit their 8in opponents three times without reply.

The action off Calabria (or, as the Italians call it, Punta Stilo) was significant in revealing the Italians' likely course of action once pressed. Their air force and navy did not operate together in harmony, while the former did not control its home waters. Communication and discipline had shown deficiencies, with Italians bombing their own ships on occasion. The long-voiced naval plea for specialized aviation had been well-founded.

A more positive result came barely a week later. Aware that the British were routeing mercantile traffic through Greek waters, the Italians dispatched two light cruisers to operate against it from the Dodecanese. Having left Tripoli in the evening of 17 July, these were entering the Aegean from the west when, at 0620 on the 19th, they sighted four British destroyers steaming on a reciprocal course close under the Cretan coast. This half-flotilla (*Hyperion*, *Ilex*, *Hero* and *Hasty*), together with *Havock*, was operating with the Australian light cruiser *Sydney*. By coincidence, they were seeking to disrupt Italian shipping. *Sydney*'s captain, J. A. Collins, had detached the four on an anti-submarine sweep and they were deployed in line abreast when the seaward ship sighted the two Italians. As the latter could both out-run and out-range the average British destroyer, all four turned sixteen points together and worked up to maximum speed to fall back on *Sydney*. The Australian, initially forty miles distant, closed at best speed: Collins was concerned that the enemy might be 8in cruisers. This fear was dispelled as 6in splashes bloomed around the fleeing destroyers.

The Italian admiral, Casardi, considered that the British disposition might represent the van of a larger force. Suspicious, he steered more to the northward, unwittingly towards the hurrying *Sydney*. By 0800 Casardi, becoming bolder, turned to starboard to shorten the range, his shooting hampered by smoke and indifferent visibility. Then, with Cape Spada on Crete in sight some twelve miles to the south, the situation changed dramatically. By maintaining radio silence, Collins achieved complete surprise, Casardi's first inkling of the *Sydney*'s presence being a straddling 6in salvo. *Giovanni della Bande Nere* was hit almost immediately.

In his anxiety, Casardi assumed the accompanying *Havock* to be a second cruiser. Believing himself pitted against 'two heavily armoured 7,000-ton cruisers [although such ships did not exist in the Royal Navy] as well as four destroyers', Casardi immediately disengaged to the south-west, making smoke. As he was zigzagging, *Sydney* was able to close the range by steering a straight course. Collins now had to shoot at the nearer and rearmost target, *Bartolomeo Colleoni*, and, at 0825, brought her to a complete standstill with a hit in a machinery space. Correctly leaving the cripple to the destroyers, the Australian pressed on after the fleeing *Bande Nere*, which she succeeded in hitting again at the cost of a shot through her own funnel. Finally, with just ten rounds left to her forward turrets, she had to abandon the chase. The *Regia Aeronautica*, having failed to detect the British in the area, now arrived in time to bomb the destroyers as they rescued *Colleoni*'s 525 survivors.

On the off-chance that the damaged *Bande Nere* might make for Tobruk, Cunningham sailed a force from Alexandria. In the event, the cruiser chose Benghazi, too far west for an interception. *Eagle* again made the most of opportunity, however, and used her Swordfish to strike at Tobruk and the Gulf of Bomba, sinking two destroyers (*Nembo* and *Ostro*) and the 2,330grt freighter *Sereno*. While the British were so occupied, the Italians seized the opportunity to run the large liners *Conte Rosso* and *Vulcania* to North Africa without incident and, virtually, without escort.

Malta still had few assets with which to interfere, and the increasing Italian boldness was related directly to pointed enquiries from the *Duce* as to when the Army intended to act. That Malta was not to be ignored, however, was demonstrated when a Sunderland of No 230 Squadron sank two Italian submarines (*Argonauta* and *Rubino*) on consecutive days. Admiral Cunningham desired to make Malta a fully operational strike base by April 1941 but, while the War Cabinet approved, the requisite bomber and fighter squadrons just could not be spared from the United Kingdom. His request for more capable ships was met to a degree, and these were to be sent along with *matériel* for both Malta and Alexandria. The Prime Minister pressed hard for two 'mechanised transport' ships to be passed directly to the Delta with fifty infantry (or 'I') tanks to equip an armoured brigade in Egypt. Stressing the uncertainty of when the attack on Egypt would develop, and the possibility of German involvement, Churchill strongly minuted both the First Sea Lord (Admiral of the Fleet Sir Dudley Pound) and the First Lord (Mr A. V. Alexander) on 13 August 1940 but, to the Premier's disgust, Pound considered the risk too great, incurring a three-week delay by insisting on sending them around the Cape. This big operation, code-named 'Hats', was timed for late August. During this period the *Regia Aeronautica* greatly reduced the scale of bombing on Malta, instead giving entirely unwanted assistance to its *Luftwaffe* allies in the aerial offensive against Britain.

In a similar vein, much of the Italian submarine fleet—which could have greatly inconvenienced the Royal Navy in the Mediterranean—was diverted to assist in the Battle of the Atlantic. Admiral Dönitz initially accepted the boats readily, but they soon proved to be woefully substandard. The Admiral was trying to develop group tactics, but the Italians turned up either late or not at all. So poorly were they rated that towards the end of the year, when the German U-boat strength had been reduced to just eighteen submarines, Dönitz still insisted that Italian 'assistance' be confined to waters south of the latitude of Gibraltar. While Dönitz fairly praised some individual Italian commanders, he, like

Kesselring, attributed their general lack of success to 'their natural character and martial characteristics'.

Mussolini's 'parallel war' exacerbated the poor material state of his forces and dispersed them to an excessive degree at a time when a concentated move against Malta must have succeeded. In August Italian forces moved into British Somaliland, which, deemed indefensible, was evacuated. The main effect of the loss was to complicate the task of maintaining mercantile traffic to Suez from the south—although, in practice, the occupiers made little use of their success.

Admiral Cunningham's problems increased considerably during August with the acceptance into service of the first two 15in-gun *Littorio*s. At the same time little could be done to interfere with the build-up of enemy forces in Libya. Only four ships engaged on this service had, so far, been destroyed, but a promising contribution was made by the continued stationing of *Eagle*'s Swordfish on forward desert airstrips. Without hazarding the carrier herself, they were able to add torpedo attack to the Royal Air Force's bombing. On 22 August they scored a notable success in sinking the depot ship *Monte Gargano* and the submarine *Iride* as they lay alongside in the Gulf of Bomba. The latter vessel, lately one of the 'mystery' submarines of the Spanish Civil War, had now been modified for the deployment of 'human torpedoes' from deck-mounted, pressure-tight containers. Two of these weapons had just been transferred, for a projected raid on Alexandria, when the aircraft struck.

Bombardment by Cunningham's heavy ships proved ineffective against Italian Army forces mobilizing in the coastal strip. This was due to wide dispersal and the low blast effect of the shells in the generally soft terrain. More damaging was the use of craft such as the newly arrived gunboat *Ladybird*, which could enter harbours and lay about them at point-blank range. A particularly useful foray against Bardia stimulated the foundation of a permanent Inshore Squadron. Old gunboats such as *Ladybird* dated from the earlier war and were of shallow-draught design for operation on the great rivers. Their destroyer escorts were, however, equally venerable, the Australian 'V&Ws' allocated being known affectionately as the 'Scrap-Iron Flotilla'.

On 30 August 1940 Admiral Cunningham's urgently requested re-inforcements left Gibraltar as part of the complex Operation 'Hats'. Because of geographical limitations, the major features of the movements were to be repeated on numerous occasions in the future. In company with Force 'H', the armoured-deck carrier *Illustrious* (with 22 Swordfish and twelve Fulmar fighters), the modernized 15in battleship *Valiant* and the small anti-aircraft cruisers *Coventry* and *Calcutta* were to reach the Central Narrows by dusk. At this point Force 'H' would turn back for

Gibraltar, leaving the reinforcements to press on, meeting Cunningham, with a portion of the Mediterranean Fleet, between Pantellaria and Malta. All of the newcomers had radar capable of ranging on aerial formations: the C-in-C was keen to improve the fleet's barrage fire as Italian high-level bombing was expected to increase in accuracy with further practice.

As Force 'H' was short of destroyers, four were to be 'borrowed' from the Mediterranean Fleet. One of these, HMS *Hostile*, struck a mine off Cape Bon. The Narrows were already well infested with these weapons, but, though in no danger of sinking, the ship had to be scuttled to avoid causing greater problems to the whole formation. This melancholy procedure was to become common in the Mediterranean, where both sentiment and a 'don't give up the ship' mentality were equally inappropriate. Carrier-based, radar-controlled fighters kept the *Regia Aeronautica* at a respectful distance from Somerville. Cunningham, meanwhile, moved westwards, taking the opportunity to run a three-ship convoy to Malta. Detecting this, the Italians sailed their two new battleships, in company with thirteen cruisers and 39 destroyers. Their quarry's position, course and speed were well known, as it was being continuously bombed, the cargo liner *Cornwall* being badly damaged.

When aerial reconnaissance detected the Italian fleet, Cunningham turned to close the convoy, a move construed by the enemy as his declining action. Even with two battleships, five cruisers and thirteen destroyers, he was in no strength to seek a fight, although *Eagle*'s presence was a bonus. The coming of darkness decided events, the Italians not being observed again until they were well on their way back to Taranto. In great strength, they had deservedly missed an opportunity, citing heavy weather and poor reconnaissance as reasons. Contrasting with this caution, Somerville turned Force 'H' on to a course that threatened Naples, striking Cagliari with *Ark Royal*'s aircraft on 1 September. To confuse the enemy further, two destroyers generated dummy radio traffic from a position north of the Balearics. The deception covered a stop-over at Malta by the reinforcements, both to refuel and to offload guns for the island's anti-aircraft defences. By the early hours of 2 September Cunningham was headed for base at Alexandria. Typically, he split his force and steered north and south of Crete to strike at enemy airfields. Honours were about even, for, although an attacking Italian MAS (motor torpedo boat) was sunk by the destroyer *Ilex*, four Swordfish were lost to Italian fighters. The poor performance of the 'Stringbags' quickly barred them from their strike role against defended targets.

Operation 'Hats' successfully delivered both reinforcements and 40,000 tons of supplies, but Churchill was scathing of senior officers who had prevented the direct shipment of the 'I' tanks to Egypt. The Prime

Minister also delivered a lengthy memorandum to Admiral Cunningham on the merits of employing his new strength to strike rapidly at the Italians before the Germans laid hands on their war machine, when 'the picture will be very different'.

With French airspace no longer accessible, aircraft for the British Near East build-up were flown across the trans-African route pioneered pre-war between Takoradi and the Sudan. Workshops assembled aircraft from crates brought in by sea and tested them. Ferry pilots then flew them 3,700 miles to the Delta along a string of airfields. Between September 1940 and October 1943 over five thousand were thus passed.

The RAF in Egypt was still poorly equipped and below strength. The AOC, Air Chief Marshal Longmore, had been promised monthly a dozen of each of his main types of aircraft. Attrition in desert conditions, however, was proving alarmingly high, with an average of one write-off per day without any major combat taking place. Higher-performance American aircraft, ordered originally to French account, were promised, but, for the moment, it appeared that Longmore would remain significantly under strength. In order to reconnoitre Italian ports and disrupt the Italian convoy routes, it remained urgent to base suitable aircraft on Malta.

Between June and September 1940, the enemy successfully delivered nearly 150,000 tons of supplies without loss. By routeing their convoys to the west of Sicily and thence via the Tunisian banks, the Italians showed the British 'O', 'P' and 'R' class submarines to be totally unsuitable for their task. Although the latter's losses on this phase outweighed their achievements, however, they obliged *Supermarina* to devote over one-third of its destroyer strength to escort duties.

On the Libya/Egypt border, the Italian preparations were so leisurely that the British discounted any military move before late September. Originally, the *Duce* had no designs on Egypt, intending to hold the east and west Libyan frontiers against the British and French in a purely defensive posture (in Balbo's words 'honourable resistance'), but, with the unanticipated French collapse, the forces to face the British could be effectively doubled. Mussolini then complicated matters by indicating an intention to strike also at Greece. His ally (with plans of his own) advised him earnestly to concentrate his limited strength in the major theatre only and even offered armoured units to assist the Italians in North Africa. They were refused, and an alternative suggestion, that, if effort had to be divided, it should be split between attacks in Libya and against Malta, was likewise turned down.

Marshal Balbo's successor, Graziani, was a seasoned colonial campaigner who well understood the importance of logistics: these, rather than sheer numbers, would decide the outcome in North Africa. With the

Germans he agreed on the necessity for control over the sea routes and air superiority over the combat zone. These requirements were not, of course, easily met and this problem, together with the directive to attack Egypt at the time the United Kingdom was invaded by the Germans, meant that affairs stagnated. Graziani was desperately short of transport, and few of his 140,000 men could be used in the manoeuvre warfare best suited to the desert. It was as obvious to General Wavell as to Graziani that the latter would have to advance quickly the 120 miles to Mersa Matruh, the nearest port and railhead. It was here, well supplied, that the British thus intended to fight.

The Italian commander's leisurely preparations were jolted on 7 September by the *Duce*'s ordering him to attack 'in two days' time', on pain of being dismissed. Increased activity resulting from this directive brought about Royal Air Force attacks on dumps, airfields and communications. These could only delay the assault, and Italian forces moved into Egypt on 13 September. Could they have seen it, the British would have been cheered considerably by Ciano's diary entry: 'Never has a military operation been undertaken so much against the will of the commanders'.

THREE

The Opening Round

September 1940 to December 1940

AS GRAZIANI crossed the frontier wire into Egypt on 13 September 1940 he had supplies for three full days and a logistics system inadequate to sustain him. He was 400 miles from the Delta. He did not enjoy air superiority and relied on convoy routes, vulnerable because Italian aircraft and submarines were being diverted to other theatres. Even so, the British Army's intention to let him advance to Mersa Matruh before opening battle was popular neither with the Royal Navy nor the Royal Air Force as, from that area, the Italians could bomb the Delta with fighter cover. As it happened, Graziani moved no further than Sidi Barrani. Concerned about his supply situation, he still had to request *Supermarina* to suspend shipments temporarily as Tripoli and Benghazi were crammed. The problem lay in moving it forwards.

Churchill's message of 8 September caused Cunningham considerable irritation. It implied that he needed 'prodding'. In a strongly worded letter to Pound, the C-in-C stated that vital aerial reconnaissance support 'fell far short' of necessary standards and that fleet operations were 'drastically curtailed' by a dearth of destroyers. Many of those not under repair or refit were being used to cover slow convoys, because no specialist escorts had been sent to Alexandria. He pointed out that two convoys per month would be necessary to build up Malta as intended. For this he would need to curtail other activities, in order to 'scrape together' sufficient destroyers. With inadequate repair facilities, he was in 'constant anxiety' that one of his capital ships would suffer damage. He faced a newly reinforced Italian Fleet, its submarines and a massive mining effort on its part in the Central Narrows. Cunningham needed no exhortations from London. He was doing his utmost with what he had, insufficient through years of government neglect. The Prime Minister was also indulging in his unfortunate habit of interfering with the decisions of the commander on the spot.

Because the Italian Army was reluctant to leave the coastal road, the Royal Navy had useful opportunities to make itself a nuisance. Thus, on 15 September, a powerful force raided Benghazi. Swordfish from

Illustrious sank the destroyer *Borea* and two merchantmen by torpedo. They also laid magnetic mines, and the Italians, unable to counter them, lost the destroyer *Aquilone* to one. The operation was marred when the cruiser *Kent*, detached to shell Bardia, was torpedoed in moonlight by an enterprising Italian aircraft. It had only just been accepted by the enemy that, following the success of the British Swordfish, a specialist torpedo-carrying flight would need to be established.

Towards the end of the month the British War Cabinet showed its nervousness regarding French naval units still 'at large' under personnel loyal to the provisional government at Vichy. Operation 'Menace' was mounted against Dakar in Senegal with the major objectives of neutralizing the incomplete 15in battleship *Richelieu* and preparing the way for occupation by a 'Free French' landing force under General de Gaulle. Although 'Menace' did not directly affect the Mediterranean war, it showed that the British still apparently harboured designs against French overseas territories and certainly against their ships. It also gave the Germans a pretext for taking over French territorial ports and airfields in North Africa on the grounds of 'protection'. That they did not do so may have been due either to lingering hopes that Vichy could still be recruited to the Axis cause or, more simply, to a lack of appreciation of the potential of such bases to influence events.

While the 'Menace' ships were still at sea, a force of three French cruisers and three 'super-destroyers' passed westwards through the Gibraltar Strait. The Gibraltar-based Flag Officer Commanding, Admiral Sir Dudley North, had been forewarned of the movement, but London assumed, wrongly, that the French had got wind of the pending operation against Dakar. Admiral North's relations with the Admiralty were strained. He had, unwisely, criticized them following the Oran affair and had received a reprimand. He remained reluctant to engage French forces and, lacking any precise directive regarding his actions on encountering them, took the view that, if the Admiralty wanted the squadron intercepted, it would instruct him to do so. No such instructions could, in fact, be forthcoming as London was dealing with a particularly large backlog of signal traffic. Thus, when the destroyer *Hotspur* encountered the French approaching the Strait at high speed and decided to shadow, her captain was ordered to break off after barely an hour.

When the First Sea Lord caught up with the decodes, he immediately recognized the implications for 'Menace'. Again incensed, he ordered Somerville to take off after the French with all dispatch. It was, of course, too late, but, fortunately, the French were bound on innocent business. Like Troubridge after the '*Goeben* Affair' of 1914, North was moved by an irate Admiralty into virtual obscurity, but the matter engendered high feelings in the Fleet.

Admiral Cunningham had been obliged for a while to watch the French force at Alexandria, understandably apprehensive at the Dakar operation. It was fortunate that the C-in-C had good working relations with the French admiral Godfroy, and that 'Menace' was eventually abandoned. Godfroy actually told Cunningham that, should their countries go to war, the ships would be scuttled rather than resort to open hostilities.

Graziani's hiatus at Sidi Barrani was seen as only temporary, and means were sought to interrupt his supply routes to deter further movements. Malta was the key, but it lacked suitable aircraft. Cunningham's request for five further cruisers and four large destroyers to form a striking force was turned down, but the War Cabinet decided to run an urgent convoy with equipment essential to building up the air defences of the island.

On 29 September 1940 the Mediterranean Fleet sailed with the convoy in an operation known, obscurely, as 'MB 5'. For once, Italian reconnaissance was up to the mark, enabling a powerful fleet including five battleships, seven heavy cruisers and four light cruisers to sail in good time. Cunningham's strength was less than half this, although he had the carrier *Illustrious* in company. While the latter's Fulmar fighters were useful in defence, her Swordfish were now outperformed even by the scout aircraft catapulted by the enemy. Aware of the odds, the British pressed on, grimly. Then, against all reason, the Italians pulled back, allowing the operation to be carried out with little further incident. A bonus of 'MB 5' was that the Australian destroyer leader *Stuart*, which had experienced mechanical trouble, encountered and sank the Italian submarine *Gondar* as she returned to Alexandria. *Gondar*, like *Iride*, had been converted for the deployment of 'human torpedoes' and had seen her operation against the British frustrated by the Mediterranean Fleet's unexpected sailing.

On 8 October the cycle was repeated with 'MB 6', the objective of which was to run four loaded merchantmen into Malta, returning with three 'empties'. As the Italian Fleet was unlikely to repeat its mistake, Cunningham sailed at full strength. Poor weather enabled the loaded convoy to be slipped into Malta without trouble, but, as the fleet awaited the sailing of the empties, the ships were spotted and reported by an Italian aircraft. Without time to sail its main strength, *Supermarina* dispatched a mixed torpedo boat/destroyer flotilla to pick off any detached units. This showed a grasp of the usual British tactic of establishing an early-warning cruiser line.

On this particular day the wing ship, some 70 miles from the main body, was the light cruiser *Ajax*. At about 0200 on 12 October, in brilliant moonlight, she spotted two strangers, one on either bow. They were the Italian *Ariel* and *Airone*, already close and about to launch torpedoes.

Even as *Ajax* flashed a challenge, *Airone* got off four gun salvos and two pairs of torpedoes. *Ajax* compensated for her slow start by blasting the Italian fatally at close range. The latter's colleague, *Ariel*, received a single 6in hit at 4,000yds and blew up. A third torpedo boat, *Alcione*, lost touch with *Ajax* but was able to rescue survivors.

Alcione's calls for assistance brought up the Italian destroyers, and the British cruiser, already struck by three 100mm shells, was suddenly hit by four 120mm projectiles from the newly arrived 'Soldati'. Nothing daunted, she responded in kind, immobilizing *Artigliere* at 3,000yds and hitting *Aviere*. Already missed by two dozen torpedoes and fighting a fire on board, *Ajax* decided to disengage. The stricken *Artigliere* was taken in tow but was sunk the following day by the cruiser *York*. *Ajax* had not benefited from her radar, which was designed to detect and range aircraft and which, in any case, had been damaged by the shock of gunfire.

This action was typical of the remorseless drip of minor reverses suffered by the Italians, which sapped their expectations of success. The C-in-C broadcast the position *en clair* to assist in the rescue of survivors, and for this act of chivalry he was chided for 'compromising [the] fleet's position' and for referring to the gallantry of the enemy! The Italians levelled the score somewhat through an aerial torpedo attack as the fleet neared Alexandria on 14 October, the cruiser *Liverpool* losing her bows. Night bombing attacks, indeed, became something of an Italian speciality, the British carriers having no night-capable fighters with which to respond.

On 28 October 1940, the eighteenth anniversary of his march on Rome, Mussolini invaded Greece from Albania. This was despite a personal visit and plea from Hitler and was a move designed to demonstrate his own independence and to prevent his Axis partner from gaining a Mediterranean foothold. Violation of Greek soil was the signal for Churchill to order the occupation of Crete, and the first British forces arrived at Suda Bay, long identified as a potential fleet anchorage, on 29 October. Military protection could be given only at the expense of Wavell's strength in Egypt, and the nearest airfield, Heraklion, was seven miles away.

Italian activity created a wealth of shipping targets in the lower Adriatic, but suitable British aircraft were too few really to capitalize on the situation, despite Longmore's valiant efforts. Even without this, however, the Italians soon began to run into the most dreadful difficulties. As usual, their army was poorly equipped, and it was now operating in hostile terrain at the onset of winter. Hitler, predictably, subjected his wayward ally to a verbal lashing, which was given added vehemence by his concerns about oil supplies. With negligible indigenous production, Germany was greatly dependent upon Romanian oil from the Ploesti region. Thanks to the Italians, however, Royal Air Force bombers could now legitimately operate from Greek fields, 'less than 500 kilometres' from Ploesti. The immediate repercussions were that Mussolini was ordered to withdraw his aircraft from Belgian airfields and to concentrate them where they were more needed; more ominously, Field Marshal Milch, the *Luftwaffe*'s Second-in-Command, submitted a comprehensive plan to deploy the specialist *Fliegerkorps X* to the Mediterranean. In Hitler's words, this sea would 'become the grave of the British Fleet in three or four months'.

In Suda Bay Cunningham gained an insecure forward anchorage; in Greece he gained an onerous new duty, safeguarding a convoy route that was permanently threatened in the flank by the Italian Fleet. The Mediterranean Fleet was, therefore, reinforced further with the battleship *Barham*, the 8in cruiser *Berwick* and the 6in cruiser *Glasgow* and three destroyers. In Operation 'Coat', these sailed from Gibraltar on 7 November 1940 in company with Force 'H' units. While *Ark Royal* used the passage eastward to raid Cagliari again, the whole force was, in turn, thoroughly bombed by the Italians. The newly introduced eight-gun Fulmar fighter had proved to be disappointingly slow, so that attacking formations could often break through. While the bombing in this case produced no actual direct hits, constant heavy shocks from near-misses caused collateral damage that was to have serious consequences.

Admiral Cunningham sailed from Alexandria both to rendezvous with the new arrivals and to act as distant cover for merchantmen bound for Greece, Crete and Malta. Force 'H', as was to be the norm, turned back for Gibraltar short of the Central Narrows. *Barham* and her accompanying ships kept on, rendezvousing with the C-in-C before stopping over briefly at Malta to offload stores and personnel. By dawn on the 11th the combined force was away and heading north-eastwards.

Italian attempts to interfere were inept. All movements from Gibraltar were immediately reported by agents ashore in neighbouring Spain, but aerial reconnaissance failed to locate any of the groups until they were too close to Malta for interception. A submarine, *Pier Capponi*, made an unsuccessful torpedo attack on the battleship *Ramillies* outside the Grand Harbour but neither destroyers nor aircraft could locate the *Barham* group: even though this formation had been spotted by Italian personnel on Pantellaria and Linosa as it passed, *Supermarina* 'could only conclude in a general way' that the British had passed within 300 miles of Taranto!

This base now played host to no fewer than six Italian battleships, which, while showing no marked readiness for major action, posed a grave threat to British interests in Greece. An apparently venerable plan to raid the port was, therefore, dusted off by Cunningham, who found an enthusiastic supporter in Rear-Admiral Lyster, whose flag was worn by the carrier *Illustrious*. Sunderlands and Marylands based on Malta provided continuous photographic intelligence on Taranto. This showed that battleships and cruisers were habitually moored in only 20–25ft (6–8m) of water, and in a line that curved parallel with the built-up area that bordered the eastern side of the Mar Grande, the near semi-circular anchorage that formed Taranto's outer harbour. The shallow water would earlier have defeated air-dropped torpedoes, but this limitation had now been largely overcome. A programme to install anti-torpedo nets had been commenced but was far from complete. To seaward of the line of moorings was a breakwater; from this and from the mainland were lines of barrage balloons, which had been deployed in order to keep would-be bombers at a safe height.

A fire in *Illustrious*'s hangar delayed proceedings until 11 November, but the plan to hit the base with a combined force of thirty Swordfish from both this carrier and *Eagle* was frustrated when the latter had to withdraw with mechanical defects caused by numerous shake-ups. She was able, however, to top up *Illustrious*'s complement, though only 21 aircraft were serviceable on the night.

The attack was organized in two waves. Flares would be dropped continuously at the back of the town to silhouette the target vessels for the attackers, who were to approach low from seaward. The low speed and open cockpits of the Swordfish were a decided asset in that the aircraft could be steered around and between the balloon cables. A bombing raid was to be synchronized, against targets in the inner harbour. This was designed both to distract the defenders and to prevent their using searchlights to dazzle the torpedo carriers.

Supermarina had discounted the probability of attack, on the unwise assumption that, should a British carrier approach to within the 180-mile radius of a Swordfish, it would be detected and destroyed. *Illustrious*, however, with only a small escort group, remained undetected by keeping close to the Greek coast before diverting to the launch point 40 miles off Cephalonia.

Of the first group of twelve aircraft, six carried torpedoes, four carried bombs and two flew with a combination of bombs and flares. They took two hours to cover the 170 miles to Taranto, which was clearly marked by Italian flak, firing long before the aircraft arrived. At about 2300 the group split, and, as intended, the diversionary activities attracted the Italians' attention. The six torpedo carriers, approaching from the west unobserved, broke into two groups and descended to only 30ft. Popping up over the breakwater, the leader, Lt-Cdr Williamson, hit *Conte di Cavour* forward, on the port side. His attention diverted, however, the pilot touched the surface and crashed, both he and his observer surviving. Just one minute later the new *Littorio*, about 1,100yds (1km) distant, was hit simultaneously on the starboard bow and port quarter, suggesting one success from each sub-flight. The remaining three torpedoes either hit the bottom or fired prematurely.

An hour later, with the Italians still tackling damage in the town, the second wave arrived. Five torpedo aircraft, a bomber and two flare-droppers adopted repeat tactics. They were successful in putting a torpedo into the starboard side of *Duilio* and two more into the unfortunate *Littorio*, only one of which exploded. One aircraft was shot down, probably by the cruiser *Gorizia*. The cruiser *Trento* and the destroyer Libeccio were hit by bombs that failed to explode. Although the 18in aircraft torpedo lacked the punch of the standard 21in version, it was sufficient. *Cavour* took five hours to settle on to the shallow bottom, at which point her superimposed main battery guns were level with the surface of the water. Despite the fact that the ship had been modernized, her inadequate subdivision had allowed progressive flooding, and she would be unserviceable until 1944. Both *Duilio* and *Littorio* ended with their bows on the bottom. Each was back in commission within six months, but the Italian Navy had lost its fast-reaction battleship force as the four remaining units were sent north for safety.

Operation 'Judgement', as the attack was named, was pronounced a great success by Cunningham: 'Twenty aircraft inflicted more damage upon the Italian Fleet than was inflicted upon the German High Seas Fleet in the daylight action at the Battle of Jutland'.

Deteriorating weather caused a planned repeat attack to be cancelled. It was certainly risky even to entertain the idea of keeping the carrier group on the enemy's doorstep, and it is likely that the lumbering Swordfish would have suffered severely in a second assault. 'Judgement' decisively shifted the balance of power in the Mediterranean, but the operation did not, as has been suggested, provide the inspiration for the Japanese attack on Pearl Harbor: this, staged a year later, was already thoroughly planned, and Taranto only confirmed its feasibility.

While the carrier force was attacking Taranto, three light cruisers, *Ajax*, *Orion* and Sydney, together with two destroyers, slipped unnoticed through the Strait of Otranto and into the Adriatic. Under the command of Vice-Admiral H. D. Pridham-Wippell, who had relieved Tovey as Commander, Light Forces, the group had been detached to look at the Italians' Brindisi–Valona convoy route. Four Italian cruisers were based at Brindisi, but safeguarding the Italian coast against surprise moves was no easier than protecting the English coast, which the Royal Navy had often found to its cost.

At 0130 on 12 November, at about the time when *Illustrious*, well to the south, was preparing to fly-on her second wave and withdraw, Pridham-Wippell, still undetected, reached the northern limit of his sweep and turned. Almost immediately he encountered a darkened group of ships. It was an empty four-ship convoy, heading west, escorted by an armed merchant cruiser (AMC) and the elderly torpedo boat *Nicola Fabrizi*. All four merchantmen, totalling about 17,000grt, were sunk and the escort was damaged. The AMC escaped.

Although the war at sea was developing well, events ashore gave cause for endless new concerns. Romania, to Hitler's intense relief, threw in her lot with the Axis. Furthermore, following the signing of the Russo-German pact of friendship, Stalin began to look southwards at what were referred to as 'lost' territories, much to the alarm of the Turks, who well comprehended Soviet ambitions to control the Black Sea exit. Anthony Eden, the British Secretary of State for War, was on a mission to GHQ Middle East. His stay was punctuated by forceful telegrams from the Prime Minister, who was desperately anxious lest Turkey were invaded or joined the Axis. Much to the concern of the joint C-in-Cs, he obviously favoured boosting the British presence in Greece at the expense of Egypt. He was diverted somewhat by Eden returning with Wavell's plan for a counter-offensive against Graziani, drawn up with the help of General Wilson, the commander of the British Army of the Nile.

This promise of action stayed Churchill's hand for the moment, although the Premier emphasized that Germany, moving on interior lines, would always have the initiative. Hitler at this time was actually seeking 'understandings' with Turkey and Yugoslavia. Mussolini's parlous situation on the Greek Front was to be assisted during the winter months by a *Luftwaffe* wing, charged also with inconveniencing the British Fleet to the maximum possible degree. In the spring German troops would be moved through Bulgaria to assist the Italians.

As ever in time of war, the United Kingdom was experiencing an acute shortage of mercantile tonnage. Convoy cycles delayed ships, and diversions to load return cargoes were usual, while ports of entry often had difficulty coping with sudden influxes as convoys arrived. Losses, though not yet common in the Mediterranean, were already outstripping replacements. In the face of an encouraging lack of aggressiveness on the part of the Italians, Admirals Cunningham and Somerville conferred on the chances of passing a fast (16kt) convoy the length of the Mediterranean. A bonus, resulting from the Taranto raid, was that Cunningham could afford to let a hard-pressed Admiralty take back *Ramillies* and *Berwick*, together with the 'visiting' light cruiser *Newcastle*. These ships would be passed from east to west; in the reverse direction, two 'Clans' would be run as far as Malta and a single Blue Star ship would sail all the way to Alexandria. In company with the latter would be four 'Flower' class corvettes—the escorts which would enable Cunningham to release some further destroyers for fleet duties.

Codenamed 'Collar', the operation would open with the convoy passing the Gibraltar Strait by night, unobserved, linking with Force 'H' for its passage east. Most of the Italians' surface strength was now based on Naples, and Somerville considered the area of greatest risk to be the 200-mile gap between Sardinia and Cape Bon. As the enemy could possibly catch Force 'H' at a disadvantage, the *Ramillies* group (termed Force 'D') would head west only until it rendezvoused with the convoy, at a point near Sardinia, whereupon it would reverse course, reinforcing Force 'H' as far as the Central Narrows. These would be reached at dusk, Forces 'D' and 'H' then heading back in company for Gibraltar, leaving the convoy to proceed to Malta with a Mediterranean Fleet destroyer screen that would arrive with Force 'D'. Complicating matters (and confusing the enemy) still further, a second convoy (MW.4) would be run to Malta simultaneously by a roundabout route to the north of Crete.

During the night of 24/25 November 1940, therefore, in company with a pair of cruisers carrying RAF personnel, the 'Collar' convoy passed Gibraltar. This was unreported, but the sailing of Force 'H' was known immediately to *Supermarina*. When, on the following day, MW.4 and a sizeable proportion of the Mediterranean Fleet were sighted near Crete, the Italians recognized a large-scale operation in progress and sailed a powerful force from Naples and Messina. Under Admiral Campioni were two battleships, six heavy cruisers and four flotillas of destroyers. As foreseen by Admiral Somerville, these were to rendezvous south-west of Sardinia by the morning of 27 November.

This day dawned calm and clear. At 0800 Somerville himself was about 100 miles south-west of Sardinia's southern capes and some 25 miles north-east of his convoy. Toiling along some ten miles astern of this formation were the four 'Flowers'. Air searches conducted from Malta and from *Ark Royal* had not yet reported anything of the enemy. Somerville, expecting air attack as the day wore on, closed the convoy to give it anti-aircraft fire support as required. He was unaware that one of *Ark Royal*'s aircraft had just sighted Italian cruisers and destroyers south of Sardinia, neither did he ever receive a report from a Malta-based Sunderland which had found Campioni as early as 0630. At 1005 the news from the *Ark Royal* aircraft had Somerville bring Force 'H' round on to a north-easterly heading. He had not yet linked with Force 'D' and was closing with a greatly superior opponent, distant some sixty miles.

As further reconnaissance reports began to amplify the disparity in opposing strengths, *Ramillies* and her group at about 1130 made a timely appearance. Admiral Somerville packed off the convoy in a safer south-easterly direction, towards the Tunisian coast. His five cruisers he formed in line abreast, ahead of the battlecruiser *Renown* and the destroyers. All worked up to maximum speed.

Campioni knew nothing of the convoy, nor of the presence of *Ark Royal* and Force 'D'. Assuming himself faced only with Force 'H', at less than full strength, he felt justified in seeking a fight, in accordance with the cautious post-Taranto guidelines that had been given to him. Just before midday, however, one of his own catapult aircraft reported both Force 'D' and the carrier. Despite being almost in sight of the Sardinian coast and its airfields, Campioni considered himself outclassed and, at 1215, ordered his force to disengage on an easterly course. This instruction had hardly been executed when the opposing sides came into visual contact.

From the bridge of *Renown*, Somerville could see two enemy cruiser squadrons. These, remaining separated, fell back on their battleships to the north. *Renown* opened at 27,000yds (over 15 miles) and even *Ramillies* managed a few salvos. Only the destroyer *Lanciere* was damaged, being fortunate to survive two heavy-calibre hits and a long tow home. The Italian cruisers could range only on the British cruiser line, and they kept it under an accurate fire. *Berwick*, the only 8in unit, lost 'Y' turret, not bearing at the time. The remaining ships were 6in 'Towns' and, of these, *Manchester* led a particularly charmed life by dint of 'salvo-chasing'.

At 1244 *Ark Royal*'s Swordfish delivered an unsuccessful torpedo attack on Campioni's battleships, nevertheless delaying them sufficiently for the British cruisers to make visual contact. The latter then immediately turned back to draw the Italians on to the British heavy units. This obvious ruse was ignored, Campioni maintaining his north-easterly course.

Following a final, unsuccessful bomb and torpedo strike by the carrier's aircraft, Somerville lost contact with the retreating enemy at 1351. He was conscious of how far he had strayed from the convoy. His quarry was bent on escape and his proximity to enemy airfields was underlined by the commencement of high-level bombing. Neither gunfire nor *Ark Royal*'s Fulmars made much difference to this: the bombing was accurate, and the carrier was severely shaken by two bombs 'within ten yards'.

From this point the operation was uneventful, the convoys and Forces 'D' and 'H' arriving unscathed. Haunted by the spectre of Taranto and lacking faith in his air support, Campioni had operated with excessive caution even 30 miles off his own coast. It was already apparent to the British that Italian surface forces, in general, lacked the necessary aggressive edge—the urge to go in and win.

The lack of a clear-cut victory was a disappointment, but it came as a shock when Admiral Somerville, even before tendering his report, heard that his conduct of the action was to be the subject of an Admiralty inquiry. He had observed his given priorities and seen them through. That his still-inexperienced carrier aircraft had been unable to slow the fleeing enemy could hardly be laid at his door. His C-in-C fully endorsed his actions, making no bones about his displeasure that Somerville should ever be called to account. In the event, the Board of Inquiry fully exonerated him of any charge of lacking offensive spirit. He had discharged his obligations to the letter, and only London emerged from the business looking less than adequate.

Both sides in the Western Desert were being well served by their respective navies and mercantile marines. By the end of November 1940 the Axis were receiving supplies at a rate of nearly 50,000 tons per month. Submarines and coasters were being pressed into service to aid the creaking logistics organization by using forward ports such as Bardia and Tobruk. Losses in transit to North Africa amounted to barely three per cent although Italian mercantile losses now totalled 53 ships of 109,000grt. Submarines had accounted directly for nearly 20 per cent of the tonnage total destroyed and, indirectly, for much of the 25 per cent lost on mines. A high proportion of mines laid were delivered by aircraft, however, and the credit must be shared. Enemy convoys were not passing unscathed, but they were far from being defeated in their objectives. Malta had to be strengthened to achieve this aim.

A massive build-up of personnel in the Delta was brought about by running fast liner convoys from the United Kingdom to the trans-shipment ports of Cape Town and Durban, and from Australasia to Bombay. Slower vessels operated a continuous shuttle between the trans-shipment ports and the Delta by way of the Red Sea and Suez Canal. For the seventeen weeks preceding the opening of the British counter-offensive in December 1940, sea power increased military strength in Egypt at the rate of 1,000 personnel per day together with vast quantities of cargo of all types. At this time, still-neutral American shipping was prohibited from proceeding beyond the Gulf of Aden, defined as the boundary of the 'war zone'.

For the most part the Red Sea was quiet, but, during October, a large, 32-ship, Bombay–Egypt convoy was attacked at night by four Italian destroyers based at Massawa. With an *ad hoc* close escort of only five sloops and ocean minesweepers, the merchantmen were fortunate to have the distant support of the New Zealand cruiser *Leander* and the destroyer *Kimberley*. The 6in fire of the cruiser broke up the challenge and caused the Italians to seek shelter among the many islands that here fringe the African coast. One, *Francesco Nullo*, was damaged sufficiently severely to necessitate her being put aground. In attempting to close and finish the job, *Kimberley* was hit by a shore battery and required towage to Port Sudan. Royal Air Force Blenheims put *Nullo* beyond repair, but the threat posed by the remaining Italians was such that they had eventually to be eliminated.

Little-used pre-war, the port of Suez was beyond the range of enemy bombers and hence was rapidly developed by the British. Air Chief Marshal Longmore also received during the final four months of the year a total of 41 Wellingtons (then classed as heavy bombers), 85 Blenheim IVs (medium bombers) and 87 Hurricanes, though attritional rates in desert conditions continued to be disturbingly high. Longmore, besides operating against Graziani, could see an imminent requirement for involvement further south on the Sudanese borders. He had already parted with five squadrons to assist in Greece and, when the winter stalemate was broken, could foresee a demand for more.

The Greeks were well aware that a British air presence would be used not only against the Italian Front but also against the sources of Romanian oil for Germany. While the latter had, as yet, betrayed no designs on Greece, such a threat against her vital oil would, as in the case of Japan, likely trigger a vigorous response. British aircraft were, therefore, not stationed in the sensitive northern territories of Greece but were obliged to operate from Lemnos, an island used 25 years earlier in the Dardanelles campaign. It was still only 400 miles from here to Ploesti, a point not lost on the *Führer* who, on 11 November, directed that plans be prepared for an invasion of Greece.

Mussolini's attitude at this juncture appears ambiguous. Dug-in on Egyptian soil, his army was sited at the head of a precarious logistics line. Its enemy was growing in strength by the day and had short supply lines and powerful air support. Mersa Matruh and its facilities had to be taken as a vital prerequisite for further advance, but to attempt its capture would be to accept battle with the British on ground of their choosing. Instead of reinforcing Graziani to resolve the issue, the *Duce* opted for a cheap victory against the Greeks. When this, too, failed, he allowed things simply to stagnate. On the night of 7/8 December 1940 the inevitable was realized when General Wavell's Army of the Nile took the offensive.

FOUR

Offensive and Counter-Offensive

December 1940 to May 1941

MARSHAL GRAZIANI'S army had entrenched itself around Sidi Barrani in a disposition of major encampments which lent itself admirably to exploitation by imaginative attack. This operation, 'Compass', was largely the brainchild of Lt-Gen Sir Richard O'Connor, commander of the Western Desert Force. By scraping together all serviceable aircraft, the Royal Air Force, though still outnumbered two to one, was able to mount something like real suppression so that the Army, which had set up forward dumps in readiness, was able to cover ground quickly.

O'Connor had only 30,000 British and Commonwealth troops (referred to hereinafter simply as 'British troops') against 80,000 Italians, but, aided by the thick-skinned 'I' (Matilda) tanks, they punched through the enemy line early on 9 December and, wheeling northwards, caused the Italians to break and retreat. Hustling the enemy back across the Libyan frontier, in deteriorating weather, O'Connor out-ran his supply organization, his problems magnified greatly by his taking increasing numbers of prisoners. The Navy came to his aid, the Inshore Squadron running up stores and ammunition and returning with prisoners of war.

By 16 December Graziani had been pushed back to Bardia, some fifteen miles beyond the border settlement of Sollum. In what became known as the Battle of Sidi Barrani, he had lost 40,000 men and 400 guns. His forces would certainly have collapsed completely had not General Wavell made the controversial decision to halt and plunder the Army to send reinforcements to the Sudan. Italian reverses brought about top-level changes. Marshal Badoglio, Chief of Staff, smarting under indirect blame for the Greek fiasco, resigned and was replaced by General Cavellero. The Naval Chief of Staff, Admiral Cavagnari (who was known by Cunningham to keep *The Life of Nelson* on his bedside table) was dropped in favour of Admiral Riccardi. The Fleet Commander, Admiral Campioni, made way for Admiral Iachino, who, as ex-Naval Attaché in London, was respected for his tactical acumen and his knowledge of the Royal Navy. The Italian Fleet itself was reorganized into six major heavy divisions, with escorts allocated as required.

The supply route to North Africa was functioning at this time better than any other aspect of the Italian war machine, with over 29,000 troops transported by the end of 1940, virtually without loss. Growing support for Greece also obliged the British to undertake a similar exercise, and the quiet spell in the wake of Taranto allowed them to convoy a quarter of a million gross tons of shipping without loss by the end of the same year.

Admiral Cunningham was keen to strike again at the Albanian port of Valona, the Italians' trans-shipment point for their Greek operations. While the weather was too poor for *Illustrious* to make any contribution, the battleships *Warspite* and *Valiant* loosed over one hundred 15in rounds 'into Valona' during the night of 18/19 December. As the ships were engaged in indirect fire over intervening 2,000ft hills, the C-in-C doubted that he 'did much damage'. It is unlikely that the inhabitants of this occupied city would have agreed. Equally unrewarding was a simultaneous sweep along the Bari–Durazzo route by his cruisers. These now lacked *Glasgow*, damaged by two aerial torpedoes while anchored in the near-unprotected Suda Bay. On the way home, Cunningham took his flagship into Malta for a few days to give the population a boost in morale. The *Illustrious*'s aircraft, meanwhile, located a three-ship Italian convoy hugging the Tunisian coast en route for Tripoli. Two of them, grossing a useful 7,500 tons, were sunk.

During January 1941 the first three of the new 'U' class submarines were due to arrive in Malta. Of only one-third the displacement of the unsuitable 'O' boats, the 'Us' had been designed as unarmed targets but were found to be of a size well suited to the confined and often shallow central Mediterranean. They were about half the size of the general-purpose 'T' class, which were also arriving slowly to replace a total of nine losses of all types. Captain G. W. G. Simpson arrived on the island in January 1941 to relieve Captain S. M. Raw as Captain (S), the latter shifting to Alexandria. Torpedoes were in such short supply that one of Simpson's first directives was to use them against southbound (i.e. loaded) Italian shipping only.

Still lacking a surface striking force, Malta depended much on the 10th Flotilla submarines based there. One of the new 'T' boats, *Triton*, had been sunk during December by the Italian torpedo boat *Clio* while working against the Albanian convoy routes. Assuming that his boats had been falling victim to mines, Raw had deployed them accordingly. However, only two (*Regulus* and *Triad*) had probably been lost in this way; the remainder had succumbed to Italian anti-submarine forces, which were far more efficient than supposed.

At the end of 1940 Malta was defended by a single squadron of Hurricanes, against an official target of four. There was also one squadron of bombers (Wellingtons) capable of raiding ports in southern Italy. These aircraft did their best against Bari and Brindisi, through which passed the majority of *matériel* bound for the Greek front, and against Naples, the major terminal for North African convoys and the base for much of the migrant Italian Fleet. When, during the night of 13/14 December, Wellingtons damaged the heavy cruiser *Pola* in the course of a raid on Naples, an alarmed *Supermarina*, rather than risk losing another capital ship, split the Fleet between Maddalena and Cagliari, at opposite ends of Sardinia.

The opening of 1941 saw Wavell concentrating on the taking of Bardia, within whose perimeters were isolated the bulk of four Italian divisions. During the run-up to the assault on the town, the Inshore Squadron, assisted when possible by Mediterranean Fleet units, kept the enemy under pressure with a succession of surprise bombardments. The 15in guns of the old monitor *Terror* were already 'worn nearly to the limit of safety' but, in Cunningham's words, 'she [could] still bowl lobs'.

With at least three Italian submarines working on the coast at any time, to say nothing of the odd torpedo-bomber, inshore operations were not without hazard. The venerable gunboat *Aphis* solved the problem by penetrating and shooting up Bardia harbour by night, although a repeat performance brought down such a volume of fire from an irritated garrison that she was lucky to escape.

Major-General Mackay's newly arrived 6th Australian Division attacked Bardia before dawn on 3 January 1941. With Swordfish spotting, Admiral Cunningham took his three 15in-gun battleships close in to give fire support. Italian formations were 'drenched' with common shell, but efforts to use some rounds of 15in shrapnel were not a success. These projectiles, dating from the Gallipoli campaign, had recently been discovered in Malta, but they refused to burst, all the balls having rusted together!

After a brisk fight, Bardia fell on 5 January. Over 40,000 prisoners were taken, together with 130 armoured and 'several hundred' wheeled vehicles. By the following day the Army had begun to invest Tobruk. This speed of advance could be supported only by the Navy moving forward stores of all kinds and removing prisoners to rear areas. The Royal Air Force also controlled the skies, largely because the *Regia Aeronautica*, unnerved by the rapid movement, chose to work from rear airfields, considerably reducing the endurance of its fighters over Tobruk. An essential component of the Tobruk defences was the modernized, 10,000-ton armoured cruiser *San Giorgio*. The ship had eight 150mm (5.9in) guns protected by 200mm (7.9in) armour and had been fitted with a comprehensive anti-aircraft armament and directors. She had already withstood numerous aerial attacks and had gained a reputation for invulnerability.

Before daybreak on 21 January 1941, under cover of a diversionary bombing raid on the town, the Australians broke from their start line and through the perimeter defences. Infantry followed behind the lumbering 'I' tanks under tactical air support. After little more han 24 hours, Tobruk fell, only little damaged by demolition. The 'Scrap-Iron Flotilla', waiting outside for *San Giorgio* to break out, was frustrated by her being blown up at her moorings. The 25,000-strong garrison that capitulated included 2,000 trained seamen. Within 48 hours naval clearance teams had Tobruk ready to receive its first shipments of supplies.

Graziani now presided over a general retreat. By 29 January the Australians had taken Derna, and two days later the Italian commander told the *Duce* of his intention to withdraw totally from the bulge of Cyrenaica to behind prepared defences east of Tripoli. By this means he would keep his army intact. O'Connor, not of course knowing his opponent's intention, obtained Wavell's agreement to an armoured thrust across the chord of Cyrenaica. This epic passage, non-stop across broken and hostile country, found the weary British astride the coast road at Beda Fomm on 5 February. They had cut off the Italian Army. Though they enjoyed an immense superiority in numbers, the Italians allowed themselves to be halted, then harried from the flank. For two days they failed to break through the British block while, pushed from behind by the advancing Australians, more kept arriving. On 7 February Benghazi was taken, and soon afterwards the Italians gave up. General O'Connor's XIII Corps, just two under-strength divisions, had, in the ten weeks since Sidi Barrani, accounted for the Italian 10th Army, comprising nine divisions organized in four corps. It had advanced 500 miles, had suffered 500 dead but had taken 130,000 prisoners. Admirably supported by the Royal Air Force, O'Connor would logically have maintained his momentum. There was apparently little to prevent him sweeping Graziani clear through Tripolitania and out of North Africa—except politics.

Prime Minister Churchill viewed the Balkans as the route back into mainland Europe but was troubled at the prospect of a Bulgarian collapse and the commencement of the threatened German assault against Greece. Backed by General Smuts (the South African Prime Minister) and the Chiefs of Staff, the Premier ordered Wavell and Longmore to Athens to offer military assistance. 'We expect and require,' said Churchill, 'prompt and active compliance with our decisions, for which we bear full responsibility'.

General Metaxas, in contrast, was bleakly realistic in his opinion that any expeditionary force sent by the British would be large enough to induce the Germans to join the Italian offensive in Greece without being of sufficient size to guarantee success. Wavell reported that the proposal was a 'dangerous half-measure'. His commitments already included the containment of the Duke of Aosta's forces in Abyssinia, a responsibility that was also progressing well. Allied with Metaxas's refusal of aid, this led the War Cabinet to give O'Connor leave to push on with his advance, at this time to secure Cyrenaica and the forward part of Benghazi. The Cabinet still entertained no plan to secure Tripolitania and thus deny the Germans any foothold in support of their ally: on the contrary, they saw the taking of Benghazi as being an end in itself, freeing forces to undertake the seizure of the Dodecanese. Such an operation, even if successful, would have had little effect on the campaign and would have involved the Royal Navy in a hazardous forward support role.

Hitler's planned move against Greece (Operation 'Marita') had, because of prolonged severe weather, been delayed from February to April 1941. This was a matter of consequence as the next major military move, that against the Soviet Union (Operation 'Barbarossa'), had been timed for May. Greece, Turkey and Soviet Russia were all in a state of apprehension at the Axis's real motives when suddenly, on 29 January, Metaxas died. Alexander Koryzis, his successor, lacked his sturdy independence and quickly reopened discussions with the British. The latter considered the ejection of the Italians from Tripolitania to be a requirement subordinate to that of preventing Axis domination of the Balkans.

In mid-February, O'Connor's men were halted at El Agheila. In one of the most short-sighted strategic decisions of the war, 100,000 of the battle-hardened troops were earmarked for transfer to Greece. Wavell himself expected a German expeditionary force at any time but believed that it could not prepare itself for an offensive before May. If only he had pressed on to take Tripoli, the Germans would not have been able to land in the first place. In Cyrenaica, the British presence was to be reduced to defence and administration and, on 24 February 1941 the War Cabinet gave the go-ahead for the move into Greece.

Admiral Raeder had, without luck, endeavoured often to convince Hitler of the significance of the Mediterranean. Another experienced voice, that of Vice-Admiral Weichold, the German naval liaison officer in Rome, stressed the benefits of suppressing Malta and occupying Crete. German military advisers, dispatched to North Africa, continued to report in the most depressing terms of the Italian military state. Nothing less than four panzer divisions would be of much use and, because of logistics difficulties, these would need to replace Italian formations rather than complement them. Predictably, the Italians were affronted and refused any offer of assistance.

During December 1940, the *Luftwaffe* was underemployed, and it was agreed to dispatch *Fliegerkorps X*, a specialist anti-shipping group, to Italy. This force, of 120 Ju 88 and He 111 bombers, 150 Ju 87 ('Stuka') dive-bombers and 40 Me 110 long-range fighters, was to be based at southern Italian and Sicilian airfields, but it was also to use Tripolitanian airstrips to attack British naval forces and their bases.

With top-level German observers continuing to report scathingly every aspect of the Italian military machine, Hitler insisted on a meeting with Mussolini. This was held at Salzburg on 19/20 January 1941 and one outcome was the Italian leader's agreement to a German 'blocking force' being sent to assist in Libya. While the *Führer* was not particularly concerned with the fate of North Africa, he well appreciated that its loss would be a blow that would almost certainly result in his ally pulling out of the war.

On 4 February plans for a large-scale intervention (Operation *'Sonnenblume'*) were put in train. A complete armoured division was to be committed, as *Fliegerkorps X* reduced Malta to impotence. General Erwin Rommel was summoned from leave and informed of his new command, which by the end of May 1941 would comprise a panzer and a motorized division. He would be subordinate to Graziani. Rommel arrived in Tripoli on 12 February, just four days after the British had halted at El Agheila. He found that Graziani had been relieved by General Gariboldi. The latter, already conditioned to defeat and retreat, was given a stiff pep-talk. German advance units, due shortly, would ensure that the British progressed no further. Not only was Tripolitania defensible, but the enemy would be pushed back into Cyrenaica as soon as opportunity offered. This course obviously exceeded the German commander's brief but, in believing that he would maintain only a defensive stance, both the British and his own High Command had misjudged the man.

Early in January 1941 the Royal Navy conducted another double convoy operation ('Excess'). Four dry-cargo ships were to be run from the western end, one of them for Malta, the remainder for Piraeus. Simultaneously, two more dry-cargo ships were to be sent to Malta from Alexandria and eight 'empties' brought out. Attached to the Alexandria movement was to be a cruiser/corvette group for Suda Bay, accompanied by a fleet oiler.

The eastbound convoy passed Gibraltar on 6 January. Its close escort (Force 'F') comprised the new anti-aircraft cruiser *Bonaventure* and four destroyers. It was overtaken the following day by Admiral Somerville's Force 'H', providing distant cover. Two cruisers, meanwhile, sailed from Greece at high speed with Army personnel for Malta. These, *Gloucester* and *Southampton* (Force 'B'), offloaded their passengers and sailed again immediately, joining the eastbound convoy as it passed the meridian of Tunis. At this point a first aerial attack, by Italian aircraft, was beaten off by *Ark Royal*'s fighters. At dusk on the 9th, as the convoy approached the Narrows, Force 'H' turned back, leaving Rear-Admiral E. de F. Renouf in

Gloucester as Senior Officer. The group passed the Narrows without incident during the hours of darkness, meeting Admiral Cunningham, who had safely delivered his own pair of merchantmen, on the 10th.

Cunningham's group (Force 'A') was a powerful one, with two battleships, the carrier *Illustrious* and eight destroyers. As it grew light, and the eastbound convoy was expected to appear, the C-in-C was surprised to see gun flashes. The convoy had first been found by a pair of Italian torpedo boats, *Vega* and *Circe*, which, unwisely in the conditions, elected to attack. Their torpedoes missed, but then, in the lumpy sea that was running, the small and lightly built Italian vessels found themselves unable to outrun *Bonaventure*. *Vega* was disabled and sunk but the damaged *Circe* managed to escape. Then, as Cunningham linked up, the destroyer *Gallant* ran on to a mine. Though she lost her forward end, almost to the bridge-front, she was towed to Malta by her flotilla-mate *Mohawk*. The ship was to prove beyond economical repair and her salvage deprived the convoy of the services of three anti-aircraft cruisers at a critical point.

Fliegerkorps X had put up two Stuka squadrons from Trapani to attack the convoy, their approach coinciding with a low-level Italian torpedo attack. In successfully beating off the latter, the carrier's Fulmars were brought to low altitude also, and as the Ju 87s rolled over at 12,000ft, making the carrier their target, they were met only by gunfire. Pulling out so low that some were observed to be below the level of the carrier's funnel top, the Stukas hit the ship with six 250 and 500kg bombs, four of which detonated within the hangar space. Subsequent experience in the Pacific was to see both American and Japanese carriers sunk by just one or two such hits, but *Illustrious* came through. It is usual to attribute her survival to her 3in armoured deck, but this is to ignore the fact that later carrier losses were invariably the result of uncontrollable fires. As the British carrier's deck was pierced several times, her escape may better be ascribed to her not having fuelled and armed aircraft below, and to her aviation spirit system not being ruptured.

As the ship could not operate aircraft, those that were airborne flew on to Malta, were turned around quickly and returned in good time to save her from the effects of a second strike. Working up to 17kts, *Illustrious* reached the island at 2200 that night. Cunningham's flagship, *Warspite*, had her forecastle nicked by a bomb which passed over the open bridge looking 'about the size of the wardroom sofa'. The carrier spent twelve days under emergency repair, her presence attracting many raids that were to cause much collateral damage in both dockyard and town. She left eventually on 23 January, proceeding via the Suez Canal to the United States. By the time she returned to Europe her services had been lost to the Royal Navy for a year. The single Malta-bound merchantman, the refrigerated cargo liner *Essex*, arrived safely. Although damaged by bombing at her berth, she was able to discharge her cargo.

Now lacking his carrier support, Cunningham moved eastwards during the night of the 10th/11th. He was being followed by Rear-Admiral Renouf's Force 'B', which had seen the unfortunate *Gallant* into Valletta. At about 1500 Renouf was attacked by the same group of Stukas, although he was now 300 miles from Trapani. At extreme range, the enemy used an He 111 as a pathfinder. *Gloucester* escaped with a bomb through her director tower, but *Southampton*, hit twice, suffered a severe fire in a machinery space. She had the misfortune to lose many of her key damage-control personnel in the initial hit. After four hours of intense effort the cruiser was deemed beyond salvation and was sunk by torpedo from the destroyer *Diamond*. Eighty of her crew were lost.

The arrival of *Fliegerkorps X* greatly altered the Mediterranean balance, though the unit's early inexperience was such that a significant number of aircraft were lost in the desert or at sea, owing mainly to navigational error.

Success in the Taranto raid had been attributable in large degree to a lack of Italian torpedo net defences. On 2 February 1941 Admiral Somerville used *Ark Royal*'s aircraft in an attempt to torpedo the strategically important hydro-electric dam at Tirso in Sardinia. The raid was thwarted by powerful anti-aircraft defences but left the Italians so apprehensive regarding the safety of several other important dams that all were equipped with net defences, even though these were in very short supply.

At this time, the Taranto-damaged battleship *Caio Duilio* was nearing the completion of repairs at Genoa. Somerville had had designs on the port for some time and sailed Force 'H' on 6 February. On the 8th *Ark Royal*'s Fulmars were sighted by the enemy, who assumed that Somerville was heading eastwards on yet another convoy exercise. Admiral Iachino may have been entertaining doubts, however, for he ordered his battleship and cruiser forces, from La Spezia and Messina, to rendezvous to the west of Sardinia, which placed a powerful concentration at a point where it could seriously inconvenience the numerically inferior Force 'H'. Hardly had the Italians effected a junction, however, than they heard that heavy shells were falling on the port area of Genoa. Hidden by a thick mist, Force 'H' was shooting on direction from spotter aircraft. Shore batteries responded ineffectually at dimly seen gun flashes. A reported 273 rounds of 15in, 782 of 6in and 400 of smaller calibre were fired, supplemented by magnetic mines dropped by *Ark Royal*'s aircraft. Genoa's docks spread over so wide an area that, of the fifty ships in port, only five were sunk, while *Caio Duilio* escaped damage completely. 'Overs' and 'wilds' caused much damage to the city. As the British returned, Iachino was in an excellent position to exact retribution, but a fogbound Ligurian Sea, combined with his aerial reconnaissance reporting a French convoy as Force 'H', conspired to frustrate his efforts. Undisturbed, Somerville arrived back at Gibraltar on 11 November.

On the same day that Force 'H' shelled Genoa, three small German merchantmen, together grossing less than 10,000 tons, sailed from Naples. They carried the first elements of General Rommel's expeditionary force, now termed the *Deutsche Afrika Korps* (DAK). As if to heighten the sense of urgency regarding the situation in Africa, it passed another group on a reciprocal course, carrying 5,000 civilians. Within a month, Rommel had received 120 tanks. The Royal Navy's failure to prevent the DAK's transfer to North Africa was to have immense repercussions but, as the scale of the *Luftwaffe*'s attack on Malta had resulted in surface ships being virtually withdrawn, it was unavoidable.

Although the crippled *Illustrious* had been replaced by *Formidable*, the latter was delayed at Suez by magnetic mines laid in the Canal (as at Tobruk and Malta) by He 111s working from the Dodecanese. *Formidable* used her enforced sojourn to good effect, working up her air group against the Italians in Somaliland.

Malta's strike capability was, for the moment, dependent upon submarines and aircraft. Captain Simpson's 10th Flotilla now had five of the new 'U' class, but all except one were still inexperienced. Relentless bombing of the dockyard delayed routine repair and maintenance, while crews enjoyed little respite between operations. The handful of Hurricanes that could be spared from North Africa for the island's defence were now being outclassed by *Luftwaffe* Me 109s. Simpson had particularly strong views regarding the disproportionately high numbers of the latest fighters being held on home soil long after the threat of invasion was past. He was backed by the ex-naval AOC, Air Marshal Longmore, who sent repeated submissions to London. Despite incurring official displeasure, he persevered, his reward being to be replaced by Lord Tedder in May 1942. Malta would not get her Spitfires yet, the *Luftwaffe* ruled her skies and the DAK was ferried safely to North Africa.

These facts seemed not to be understood by General Wavell, who totally underestimated German strength and capability. Lacking customary French intelligence sources, the British confirmed the German presence only on 21 February. In early March it was deemed too weak to pose any threat to Benghazi and it was considered that it would be unable to attack before the end of the month.

It was at this stage that British cryptanalysts cracked the key used by the *Luftwaffe* on their 'Enigma' coding machines. It was thus soon revealed that Rommel could move earlier than anticipated. Wavell received also an intelligence assessment that forecast the Germans first securing Tripolitania, then using it as a springboard to take Cyrenaica, from which they would threaten Egypt. Wavell, nonetheless, proceeded with the dispatch of troops and *matériel* to Greece (Operation 'Lustre'). He also inspected British dispositions in Cyrenaica and returned a worried man.

Rommel was reminded of his limited objectives by his High Command on 19 March, but, sensing the British weakness, attacked at El Agheila on the 24th. With British armoured and aerial assets stripped to support 'Lustre', and the ground held by unblooded troops, the DAK found its task simplified. On 1 April it advanced on Agedabia and by the 3rd had occupied Benghazi.

Despite being 'berated violently' by his Italian superior for exceeding his brief, Rommel put General O'Connor's earlier plan into reverse and advanced across the chord of Cyrenaica. It was now the turn of the British to beat a panicky retreat, the Germans passing Mechili on 6 April and heading on for Derna. In the course of this phase they captured O'Connor, probably the only man on his side then capable of stopping the rot. On this same day, Yugoslavia and Greece were being invaded.

A three-day rearguard action by an Indian brigade gave the Australians time to retreat into Tobruk and begin to improve its defence. On the 15th the DAK attempted to take it with a quickly organized thrust but met its first repulse. General Morshead's men had decided that the retreat had gone far enough and at Tobruk they would make a stand. By the 11th the port was totally cut off and, until 16 April, it was subjected to a series of armoured attacks, mounted with the object of opening a way for enemy infantry. All failed, mainly to excellent timing by Morshead and a superb use of artillery. Disgusted at the failure of tactics that had worked faultlessly in Europe, Rommel commenced planning in greater depth for a later offensive and drove the DAK eastwards, to Capuzzo and Sollum—virtually back to the frontier wire whence the campaign had commenced some seven months earlier.

With the timetables for 'Marita' and 'Barbarossa' already awry, the German High Command began to complain loudly at Rommel, his methods and his demands for *matériel* at an impossible time. General Paulus, a deputy to the Chief of the Army General Staff (OKH), was dispatched to evaluate the situation. With reservations, he approved Rommel's plans, but his radioed report to Berlin was read by the British. Churchill exhorted Wavell to strike first.

At considerable risk, a convoy ('Tiger') was to be run the length of the Mediterranean, to dock at Alexandria with 250 'I' tanks on 12 May. Wavell did not wait, commiting all his armoured reserves in an attack codenamed 'Brevity'. This was launched on 15 May, a triple thrust that met with early success. Rommel, however, concerned that its aim was to relieve the beseiged Tobruk, reacted boldly. For the first time in Africa the British encountered the 88mm heavy anti-aircraft gun used in the ground role in which it became respected. The DAK discovered that fighting at the head of an 1,100-mile long logistics line was fraught with problems. Both sides had difficulty in establishing the whereabouts of individual units and, indeed, identifying what could be seen. 'Brevity' did not achieve a lot, but, in view of the enemy's perceived limitations, preparations were put in hand for a repeat attack.

At a time when British armoured production was working to replace the enormous losses incurred at Dunkirk, Churchill was bold in diverting a significant number of tanks to North Africa. It is, therefore, not surprising to find him overriding the instincts of Admiral Cunningham by insisting on the running of the 'Tiger' convoy. Five fast merchantmen passed into the Mediterranean on 6 May and, escorted by Force 'H' as far as the Narrows, reached the longitude of Malta before losing its first ship. This, the *Empire Song*, was mined. Cunningham, having safely delivered four dry-cargo ships and two tankers to Malta, took over the 'Tiger' convoy at this stage, together with the reinforcements that accompanied it (the battleship *Queen Elizabeth* and two cruisers). En route, he detached the cruiser *Ajax*, with destroyer escort, to bombard Benghazi. Returning, they encountered and destroyed two small Italian merchantmen laden with motor transport sorely needed by the DAK.

The eastern leg of the 'Tiger' passage was without incident as the seasonal *scirocco* brought thick cloud 'almost down to our mastheads'. An unfortunate consequence of this easy run was that London believed that the dangers of running Mediterranean convoys had been overstated. 'Before long,' recorded Cunningham, 'the dismal truth was to be brought home to them.'

The four surviving ships discharged, from 12 May, 135 'I' tanks, 82 cruisers and 21 light tanks. These were to be used to rebuild the 7th Armoured Division. General Wavell was already being pressured by the Premier to hasten a second major offensive (code-named 'Battleaxe'). Delay was, however, inevitable. The discharge of such heavy items took a considerable time, and a large amount of repair and refurbishment was required following their long passage. Training had also to be taken into account. An interesting situation occured at this juncture: a cautious British commander was being hurried along by his High Command at the same time as his headstrong German counterpart was refusing to be reined back.

Rommel, rightly concerned that the Tobruk defences would be rapidly strengthened, staged a third attempt at its capture on 30 April. The DAK succeeded in establishing a small salient but was mauled badly by a combination of artillery and minefields well covered by anti-tank guns.

By 4 May the situation had become stalemated, with the Axis retaining its small gain but having failed in its main attack. It had incurred 1,150 casualties in its attempt and Rommel was, once again, the subject of an unfavourable von Paulus report.

In addition to denying the sea to the enemy, the Royal Navy now had to support Tobruk as well as cope with the deteriorating situation around Greece. Only destroyers had the speed to reach Tobruk, discharge and withdraw during the winter nights and, following the dive-bombing of two hospital ships, they acted also in casualty evacuation. Such a passage was often a stimulating prelude to a spell in hospital, for a casualty, if mobile, could expect to find himself manning an automatic weapon as the ship manoeuvred violently to outsmart a marauding Stuka. To the average, hard-pressed matelot, the Royal Air Force never seemed to be in evidence, but, in practice, its slender numbers were usually commited well beyond the ships' horizons.

A graphic description of such a run has been left by the First Lieutenant of the destroyer *Hotspur*. An average load was about forty tons: 'shells, cartridges, landmines, cases of bully beef and spuds by the hundred . . . onions, carrots and huge anaemic marrows . . . while now and then a few weighty objects, like spare gun barrels, were heaved aboard and lashed down on deck'. In total darkness, each destroyer would have to find the entrance to Tobruk harbour, avoid the wrecks that littered the approach and the buoys that marked the (approximate) position of air-dropped mines. Discharge could either be on to the single usable jetty or overside into barges. What was not landed within the hour stayed aboard for the return trip for, if there were any fighter escort, it could not hang around. Slower ships, such as water, fuel and vehicle carriers, had to spend the day in harbour, the trick being to resemble a wreck as closely as possible.

Losses mounted. The Australian 'Scrap-Iron Flotilla' destroyer *Waterhen* was ill-armed for defence against air attack but *Auckland* and *Parramatta* were modern anti-aircraft sloops. Ideal for the Tobruk trade were the Royal Navy's fast minelayers. They combined a powerful high-angle armament with a 40kt speed, good manoeuvrability and mine galleries well suited for cargo space. *Latona* of this class, like *Auckland*, fell victim to Italian aircraft.

Apparently unaware of the disquiet that Rommel's maverick behaviour was causing his High Command, the British War Cabinet urgently sought means of denying him the key port of Tripoli. The DAK's eastward advance had put the port beyond the effective reach of British bombers, while Malta's strike capacity was continuing to be severely eroded. Only nine Wellingtons remained on the island, always at risk of being destroyed on the ground. Malta-based Swordfish could reach Tripoli with mines, but these were not seen as likely to produce decisive results.

Admiral Cunningham was pressured by London to undertake a massive fleet bombardment but showed a marked reluctance to do so. A round trip of 1,700 miles was beyond the high-speed endurance of many of his ships, and the C-in-C held that the risks involved were not justified by likely results. As an interim measure, however, he was dispatching a half-flotilla of destroyers, to work from Malta against the convoy route from about 10 April. This measure was viewed by Churchill as insufficient. In a directive of 14 April he reminded the Admiral that his Fleet's 'prime duty' was to break the supply route between Italy and North Africa. He added, ungraciously, that 'every convoy which gets through must be considered a serious naval failure'. The Fleet was to be reinforced for the purpose while the fighter strength on Malta was to be boosted to protect them. In retrospect, it seems reasonable to ask, like Longmore and Simpson did, why, as it appeared eminently feasible, this had not been done before.

On 15 April came a War Cabinet demand that Tripoli be blocked. Cunningham had already been offered the old battleship *Centurion* for this purpose. Long disarmed and used as a radio-controlled target ship, this veteran had been mocked-up topside to resemble a *King George V* class battleship. The C-in-C had been prepared to use her, but it was to be another year before she turned up at Suez, following a round-the-Cape odyssey punctured by misfortune. Her non-availability, however, was to be no excuse for avoiding the directive: the Admiralty ordered simply that the battleship *Barham* and a 'C' class cruiser were to be sacrificed instead.

Cunningham, already faced by commitments that threatened to swamp his limited resources, was aghast. He saw the order as 'naïve . . . extraordinary . . . [and] apparently dictated by somebody who appeared to know little of [the situation] in the Mediterranean'. In the face of the greater threat of the immolation of *Barham*, the Fleet duly undertook the bombardment of Tripoli on 21 April 1941.

The passage of the bombarding force—three battleships and their supporting carrier *Formidable*—was well disguised. Two groups of warships rendezvoused with the fleet transport *Breconshire* on what looked like a routine westbound deployment to Malta. An empty, eastbound group from the island was timed to pass the main force at about dusk on 20 April. Only after darkness fell did the bombardment force head south for Tripoli, leaving the *Breconshire* to proceed with one destroyer.

For two hours preceding the bombardment, scheduled to commence at 0500, two hours before dawn, Tripoli was to be bombed by Malta-based aircraft. *Formidable*, 60 miles offshore, was to have flare-dropping Swordfish over the target at 0445, following directly after the bombing. Spotter aircraft were also to be present. As, in these pre-radar days, it would be difficult to estimate range at night, a submarine was to be ready-posted exactly four miles offshore and guide the bombarding ships with a shaded lamp.

Between 0502 and 0544, a recorded 478 rounds of 15in and about 1,500 of 6in and 4.7in were fired. The dust and smoke, illuminated by flares, combined with the close proximity of the falling salvos, made correction impossible. Much damage was thus caused to the town, comparatively little to the port. Hitting soft targets, many of the 15in shells were reported by the Italians not to have detonated. Only one ship was sunk and this, though laden with fuel and explosives, failed to blow up.

No attempt was made to hinder the Fleet's return to Alexandria, but Cunningham remained unrepentant: in his view the force had been fortunate and its luck could scarcely hold a second time. Pressure from London for the operation to be repeated was relaxed as commitments to the Greek campaign grew.

The half-flotilla of destroyers that Cunningham had recently sent to Malta had already chalked up a major success. At about noon on 15 April aerial reconnaissance reported a loaded, southbound convoy near Cape Bon. It comprised five merchantmen (four of them German), escorted by the large destroyer *Luca Tarigo* and two torpedo boats. Known as Force 'K', the four British destroyers (*Jervis*, *Janus*, *Nubian* and *Mohawk*), under the command of Captain P. J. Mack, sailed immediately. By dint of hard steaming they intercepted the enemy off Sfax in the small hours. Three of the cargo ships were sunk by close-range gunfire, the remaining pair being run on to the Kerkenah Banks. Outnumbered, the escort fought back, *Tarigo* catching *Mohawk* with two torpedoes: a third passed beneath *Jervis*. Daylight found *Mohawk* bottomed aft in seven fathoms but with her forecastle still buoyant. The torpedo boat *Baleno* was sinking in deep water and her sister *Lampo* was on the bottom in the shallows. A convoy had been effectively annihilated and over 1,750 of 3,000 embarked troops drowned.

Single, unescorted merchant ships were occasionally slipped through to Malta with, often, a better chance of survival than if convoyed. This was the reverse to the situation obtaining in the Atlantic. In the vastness of an ocean a convoy was little more detectable than a single ship. The same number of vessels, run independently, had a far higher chance of detection—a fact confirmed by hard experience. In contrast, Mediterranean convoys could not 'disappear'. Sailings from either end were invariably reported, while geography greatly limited the options for evasive routeing. The entire Sea could easily be covered by aerial reconnaissance. The nature of the opposition was also different. In the Atlantic the battle was, almost exclusively, against the U-boat; in the Mediterranean the threats came primarily from the air and from surface attack, necessitating large fleet operations. Once Dönitz was ordered to deploy submarines in the Mediterranean, the 15kt convoys required escort by destroyers rather than by the corvettes and fighters employed in the Atlantic. At this speed, however, the average destroyer's asdic was limited by noise in its chances of detecting a submarine.

Some 'independents', such as the 4,700grt *Parracombe*, were unlucky. Carrying 21 cased Hurricanes, spare parts and ground crews for Malta, she came to grief on a mine on 2 May whilst hugging the Tunisian coast. As the 'Tiger' convoy was about to be run, it would have been more practical to organize an extra fast freighter for the purpose, but, as it was, such a severe loss saw the First Sea Lord receive a waspish signal from the Prime Minister. *Breconshire*, by contrast, for long ran a charmed life. A new ship, powerfully built for the Glen Line's Far East service, she wore the White Ensign and ran regular trips with mixed cargoes, particularly ammunition and cased fuel.

Improving British intelligence was complemented by an increase in strength of No 69 Squadron's Maryland reconnaissance aircraft operating from Malta. On 23 April one reported a five-ship convoy, southbound and covered by four destroyers. Following the disaster of the previous week, the Italians provided a distant cover of two cruisers and two further destroyers. Captain Mack's destroyers sailed immediately, and prospects of a successful interception looked bright when, at 0300 on the 24th, a radar-equipped night flyer placed the destroyers only four miles from the target. The contact, however, was a solitary Italian vessel, the 3,300-ton armed auxiliary *Egeo*. She was speedily destroyed, but the convoy, still thirty miles distant, was alerted, altered course and escaped.

Four days later Mack's force was relieved by the six 'J'/'K' class destroyers of Captain Lord Louis Mountbatten's newly arrived 5th Flotilla. They were greatly needed, for the Navy was sorely stretched in other directions and, with *Fliegerkorps X* keeping Malta subdued, the Italians were running an average of over 80,000 tons per month to North Africa. Even with a loss rate of eight per cent, the Axis armies' monthly requirement of 70,000 tons was being more than met.

FIVE

Peripheral Activities

February 1941 to August 1941

PRIME MINISTER Churchill's weakness for the unorthodox, and his powerful inclinations to take the offensive wherever possible, made him highly receptive to the arguments of the veteran swashbuckler Admiral of the Fleet Sir Roger Keyes, who advocated the establishment of Amphibious Striking Forces. Their personnel were to be hand-picked from the Regular Army and Royal Marines and formed into ten 'Striking Companies'. The term adopted eventually was 'Commandos'. Once created, of course, these had to be employed, and proposals for their use caused no little dissent.

Keyes first identified the island of Pantellaria for seizure. To be sure, it lay in the Narrows, but it boasted a miniscule harbour and insufficient flat ground for an airfield of any size. Most importantly, it was dominated totally by its proximity to Sicily. Nevertheless, at a time when the nation needed a fillip to its morale, Keyes and Churchill agreed to 'do a Zeebrugge', and Operation 'Workshop' was planned. Admiral Cunningham (out-ranked if Keyes became involved) was strongly opposed to taking a scrap of land of only marginal use and then having to maintain and defend it in the teeth of enemy opposition. In this he was powerfully backed by the First Sea Lord, Admiral Pound, who pointed out that Pantellaria had caused 'very little trouble'.

Faced by such concentrated opposition, the Prime Minister was deflected, though still inclined to rate Cunningham as overcautious. Thus the question of Operation 'Mandibles', directed at the Dodecanese, was raised. The same arguments could be used here as well, but, from early 1941, increased British convoy activity across the Aegean to Greece was threatened by enemy surface forces from Leros and aircraft from Rhodes and Scarpanto. It was known that the maintenance of their garrisons in the islands was causing the Italians some inconvenience, and it was not difficult to persuade the Premier that a British naval presence in the area would be desirable. The small island of Castelorizzo, just off the Turkish coast, was identified as suitable for a motor torpedo boat (MTB) base. Early on 25 February 1941, therefore, the destroyers *Decoy* and

Hereward, accompanied by the gunboat *Ladybird*, made the short crossing from Crete and landed 225 personnel. These, welcomed by the largely Turkish community, quickly secured the island.

However, an Italian nerve seemed to have been touched, for there came an uncharacteristically vigorous response. A rapid bombing attack damaged one of the withdrawing British ships, and this was followed that night by a bombardment and landing, staged by four Italian units from Rhodes. Cunningham had to risk his destroyers again to take off those British personnel that had not already been obliged to surrender. The C-in-C was furious at such cloak-and-dagger types of warfare, involving personnel who 'apparently can't defend themselves if seriously attacked'. Chagrined, Churchill ordered the affair to be 'probed properly' but went on to criticize the Navy for withdrawing without isolating the island.

A week later, on 4 March 1941, the first 'Lustre' convoy left Egypt for Greece. The required three-day cycle was to place much extra load on the Mediterranean Fleet. Also on the 4th came the announcement that Cunningham had been created a KCB. His comment was 'I would sooner have three squadrons of Hurricanes', a sentiment expressed more in sorrow than in anger as his ships continued to be sacrificed along the Cyrenaican coast in support of the Army. Air Chief Marshal Longmore's thirty remaining serviceable fighters faced over 200 Axis aircraft at this time.

At Merano, in mid-February, senior Italian officers were informed by their ally that stronger measures would have to be taken against the Royal Navy. The Italian Fleet was already restricted by a shortage of fuel and depended on the Germans to supply its needs. Without explicitly stating their intention of going into Greece themselves, the Germans stressed that the British must be prevented from building up their strength there. *Supermarina* was cautious, as Mussolini himself had forbade the fleet to be unduly hazarded because he would need its existence in order to bargain from a position of strength at the anticipated peace conference. The Italians demanded, therefore, that *Fliegerkorps X* provide both the reconnaissance and the aerial protection that their Fleet lacked. They obtained an agreement regarding the reconnaissance and the provision of cover beyond the range of their own airfields in the Dodecanese. Further, suppression attacks on Malta were to be stepped up.

Over 100 Axis bombers were thus over Malta on 5 and 6 March. Able to muster only eleven fighters in the island's defence, the AOC, Air Vice-Marshal Maynard, had all remaining Wellingtons and Sunderlands withdrawn to the Delta for their very survival. The situation resulted in a terse exchange of notes between a concerned Cunningham and the First Sea Lord, the latter stating that the Battle of the Atlantic enjoyed overriding priority and that carriers could not be risked to fly-in more

Hurricanes. The C-in-C should, therefore, 'disabuse Longmore' of any such expectations. On 10 March the delayed arrival of the carrier *Formidable* relieved the chill somewhat.

Heightened Italian naval activity commenced on 26 March 1941 when the same two destroyers that had been instrumental in the recapture of Castelorizzo—*Crispi* and *Sella*—sailed from their Leros base with a deck cargo of six explosive motor boats. These were set afloat near the entrance to Suda Bay, whereupon they quietly negotiated the seven-mile-long inlet. Once in sight of the anchored targets, the driver of each aimed it, locked the steering and the throttle wide open and baled out quickly. Admiral Cunningham's only 8in cruiser, HMS *York*, was hit and severely damaged. Her power having failed and with her machinery spaces flooding, she was put aground. She could not be repaired by local resources and, overtaken by events, she became a total loss. Also put on the bottom was the 8,300-ton Norwegian tanker *Pericles*, much of whose valuable cargo could, however, be salvaged.

On this same night, 26/27 March 1941, the Italians sailed in force to intercept a British convoy. The plan, code-named 'Gaudo', called for a cruiser/destroyer force to sweep along the northern coast of Crete, paralleled by a more powerful group, accompanied by the battleship *Vittorio Veneto*, moving along the southern coast. Working in conjunction with German reconnaissance aircraft, they were to destroy any British shipping detected. Admiral Iachino had reason to feel confident as, only ten days earlier, the *Luftwaffe* had claimed to have torpedoed and disabled two of Cunningham's three battleships. This claim had no foundation in fact, and, indeed, the C-in-C had been alerted by a heightened level of German reconnaissance over Alexandria. Not only the *Luftwaffe* 'Enigma' codes but also the Italian naval cypher was now being read by the British, but, because it was not clear if the indicated move would be against convoys, Crete or Malta, Cunningham decided not to sail until hard evidence was available. Thus he expected the possibility of interception to be enhanced.

During the forenoon of the 27th a Malta-based Sunderland reported three Italian cruisers and a destroyer about 80 miles east of Cape Passero, steering south-eastwards. They were the ships of Sansonetti's 3rd Division, accompanying the battleship. Because of the indifferent visibility, the latter was not detected—a fact known to the Italians, who intercepted the signal from the aircraft. Admiral Cunningham and his staff were sure that something larger was afoot and, having turned back one British convoy and delayed the sailing of another, were under way at maximum strength immediately after dark on the 27th. The battleships *Barham* and *Valiant* were somewhat slowed by their flagship, *Warspite*, which was limited to only 20kts. In company was the new carrier

Formidable. Already at sea were Pridham-Wippell's light forces, including four 6in cruisers. He was ordered by the C-in-C to be south of Crete by first light on the 28th.

At about the time that the British were sailing, Iachino was seized with doubt following the earlier sighting by the Sunderland. He ordered his just-divided squadron to re-concentrate. At dawn on the 28th, therefore, *Vittorio Veneto* was thirty miles off the south coast of Crete. Some ten miles ahead of her was the heavy cruiser squadron, while the light cruisers trailed some fifteen miles on her port quarter. Two reconnaissance aircraft were catapulted at 0600 and soon reported on Pridham-Wippell, who was about fifty miles distant. Iachino instructed his heavy cruisers to contact and delay the British until the slower battleship could come up.

Dawn searches from *Formidable*, meanwhile, found all the Italian cruisers but again missed *Veneto*. As Pridham-Wippell did not appear to be unduly threatened by the enemy forces so far located, Cunningham did not react immediately. At 0758, however, Sansonetti's masts and smoke were sighted from Pridham-Wippell's flagship, *Orion*. As the British were 90 miles from their main body and faced opponents that could outrun and outgun them, their situation was not good. They immediately hauled away to the south-east to keep the range open and to draw their pursuers on to Cunningham's heavy units.

Sansonetti opened fire at 0812. From 25,000m (over 27,000yds), his 8in salvos were accurate enough to oblige *Gloucester* to weave. With the range dropping but still beyond the capacity of the British 6in guns, the C-in-C could intervene only through an air strike. Fortunately for Pridham-Wippell, his pursuers were suddenly, at 0855, recalled by Iachino. This was for the weak reason that air cover by *Fliegerkorps X* had not materialized and that British air attacks could be expected; indeed, Iachino now considered that, as no British convoys had been sighted, his mission was over. Pridham-Wippell, who should have been at the Italians' mercy, therefore reverted to a classic cruiser 'track-and-report' role, out of range on Sansonetti's quarter.

Emboldened by a continued lack of aerial activity, Iachino suddenly reversed course at 1035, hoping to catch the British light forces between his flagship's 15in guns and Sansonetti's cruisers. Within a quarter of an hour *Veneto* could be seen from *Orion* and, for the second time that morning, Pridham-Wippell fled, with 15in shell splashes towering above his smoke. Fortunately, the C-in-C had already ordered an air strike from *Formidable*. This, comprising six torpedo-armed Albacores covered by a pair of Fulmars, sighted the Italian battleship at 1058, but the aircraft's speed was so poor that they took until 1115 to gain an attacking position. This was the Albacore's combat début but, though pressed to within 2,000m, it enjoyed no success (although one definite and one probable hit were claimed). The attack did allow the hard-pressed British light forces to disengage, however, and persuaded Iachino that he should withdraw. By 1130 he was heading westwards at 25kts.

Cunningham was none too pleased with developments. Instead of being slowed sufficiently for him to catch up and finish her off in daylight, *Veneto* was 80 miles away and steaming fast. A second attack, by Crete-based Swordfish, caused no damage to the rapidly manoeuvring Sansonetti. By 1230 the British forces had concentrated and *Formidable* flew off another strike. This reached the enemy at the same time as Royal Air Force Blenheims arrived from Crete. The FAA aircraft synchronized their torpedo launches from several directions while the Italians were still distracted by the RAF. Although the lead Albacore was shot down, *Veneto* took a hit in the vicinity of the port propellers. Taking on about 4,000 tons of water, the battleship came to a halt and, still over 400 miles from Taranto, looked good for interception. Her crew worked well, however, getting power back to the starboard shafts. An initial 10kts was slowly improved to 20.

Admiral Iachino was still pleading in vain for *Luftwaffe* assistance. Lacking reconnaissance, the Italians assumed, wrongly, that Pridham-Wippell, thankful to escape, would be heading for Alexandria. Also, Cunningham's presence remained undetected, despite air strikes from aircraft that were obviously carrier-borne. Iachino therefore detached a cruiser squadron for Brindisi and gathered the remainder about his injured flagship for the passage to Taranto.

With the day wearing on, Cunningham prepared for a night engagement. At 1644 Pridham-Wippell ordered 'Ahead' at maximum speed to establish a visual link, while Captain Mack's destroyers were formed into a surface strike force. *Warspite*'s aircraft, catapulted at 1745, sent back a steady stream of data on Iachino's progress. He was estimated to be distant 45 miles and making a good 15kts. At only 20–22kts, however, the British were overhauling their quarry depressingly slowly.

A further *Formidable* strike, supported by aircraft from Crete, went in at dusk. Radio intercepts had warned the Italians, who flanked their flagship closely with cruisers and destroyers before the aircraft arrived. Despite the compact nature of the formation, its effective use of smoke, searchlight-dazzling and barrage fire all but defeated the attack. *Veneto* escaped further damage, but a torpedo found the heavy cruiser *Pola*, which was brought to a standstill.

Iachino had been informed by *Supermarina* two hours previously that radio transmissions indicated a British force some 75 miles behind. Instead of following this up with aerial reconnaissance, however, the Italians made the totally unwarranted assumption that it was only a patrol. This led to the Admiral detaching the stricken cruiser's two division mates, *Zara* and *Fiume*, to assist, covered by a pair of destroyers. The time was now 2038 and Iachino was again warned by his High Command of the proximity of British forces. Pounding up astern, meanwhile, Cunningham became apprehensive at the approach of darkness. He anticipated an all-out mêlée involving every torpedo-carrying destroyer and cruiser that the enemy could muster. Darkness and confusion could offset any local advantage in firepower, while there was always the risk of damage to the precious *Formidable*, leaving her vulnerable to daylight air attack.

The C-in-C deliberated over his evening meal and then ordered away Mack's destroyers. These disappeared, 'turning and twisting like snipe', at over 30kts into the gloom. Their quarry was now estimated to be 33 miles ahead. One trump card held by the British was the radar, albeit rudimentary, aboard *Formidable*, *Valiant* and *Ajax*. The last had repaired the apparatus damaged in the night action of the previous October and, at 2015, detected a stationary vessel at six miles' range. Cunningham, from his pilot's reports, expected to find *Veneto*, damaged by up to three torpedoes and several bombs. Pridham-Wippell, correctly, confirmed the contact and held on after the Italian main body, yet undetected.

Valiant's radar, again at six miles, also confirmed the presence of the mysterious stranger at 2210. It was calm and moonless. Extreme visibility was only 2½ miles as the three British capital ships closed in quarter line, only their forward guns bearing. Then, at 2225, two cruisers and a smaller ship were sighted visually from *Warspite*. Moving slowly from right to left, they seemed oblivious of their peril. The British turned together to starboard, forming line ahead and unmasking their after batteries. They were at a range estimated at no more than 3,800yds. At about this juncture, the disabled *Pola* sighted the dark shapes of the British and, assuming them to be her own divisional ships coming to her aid, fired a red rocket. Any hope that *Zara* and *Fiume* had of realizing their peril was sidetracked by this signal, their attention distracted.

Suddenly the night's velvety blackness was lanced by the beam of a searchlight from the destroyer *Greyhound*. Illuminated squarely, shining silver-grey, was a large Italian cruiser. The flagship's own lights snapped on at the instant of the crash of the opening salvo. Six 15in projectiles, clearly visible in the glare, followed a short, flat trajectory. Five hit simultaneously a few feet below the level of the target's upper deck. Untrained in night fighting, the Italian admiral, Cattaneo, had been totally surprised, his armament fore and aft. He had four destroyers in company, and why he had not thrown these out in a scouting line remains a mystery.

'The plight of the Italian cruisers was indescribable,' wrote Cunningham later, '[with] whole turrets and masses of other heavy debris whirling through the air.' Secondary batteries engaged the Italian destroyers, totally disabling *Alfieri* and shattering *Carducci*'s topsides. To avoid any enemy torpedoes, Cunningham then turned eight points together to starboard, releasing his four remaining destroyers to finish the job.

Captain Mack's destroyers, meanwhile, had missed an encounter with Iachino due to the latter's abrupt change of course after dark. They were still searching when, at 0030, they intercepted a signal from *Havock*, some 60 miles away, that she was in touch with a '*Littorio* class battleship'. Mack turned back at full speed, sighting a searchlight at about 0200 then passing through many floating survivors before seeing a dark, stationary form ahead. The men in the water were from *Fiume*, which had blown up at 2315. Ahead lay the sullenly smouldering hulk of *Zara*. Promptly torpedoed by *Jervis*, the wreck again erupted into flame. From *Hotspur* the scene was awe-inspiring: 'The flames seemed to make her gigantic. She was turning over gradually so that she showed us her whole deck . . . One turret was just not there, and the others were pointing heedlessly fore and aft. The bridge was enveloped in mountainous flames, and above hung a pillar of smoke, with its underpart aglow . . . Shortly afterward she rolled over and foundered.' Just two miles further on they found *Pola*, the unwitting cause of the tragedy. Still afflicted by a total power failure, she was unable even to pass a shell up from a magazine. Her colleagues' fate was about to become hers also. It was *Havock*'s misidentification of *Pola* that had brought Mack to the scene. In the quiet conditions, the destroyers were able to range alongside to remove her crew before finishing her off by torpedo.

At first light the British were able to haul many more survivors from a sea covered in oil and wreckage. Their action was curtailed by the arrival, at last, of the promised *Luftwaffe* support. As a *Formidable* search had confirmed that Iachino was now beyond interception, Cunningham signalled *Supermarina* the position of the remaining survivors and left the scene.

The Battle of Matapan, while it had not accounted for *Vittorio Veneto*, had been a resounding success. At the cost of one aircraft and crew, the Mediterranean Fleet had disposed of three heavy cruisers and two modern destroyers, with 2,400 of their crews. *Supermarina* put the blame squarely, upon *Fliegerkorps X* for its lack of support. In turn, the Germans criticized the Italian Navy on just about every count. Suspicion was mutual between the Axis partners that one or the other was responsible for leaking plans. Most importantly, the Italians became even less ready to tangle with the Royal Navy on anything like equal terms.

In ascribing the disaster largely to the presence of *Formidable*, Mussolini decreed that, within a year, the *Regia Marina* was to get carriers of its own. Two liners were put in hand for conversion, but, though named *Aquila* and *Sparviero*, they were fated never to be completed. The Italians levelled the score somewhat when, on 31 March, four days after the sinking of *York*, the submarine *Ambra* put two torpedoes into the cruiser *Bonaventure*. This useful ship, the first *Dido* class ship to be completed, sank in barely five minutes with a loss of about 170 crew.

Events ashore gathered pace. British troops in Greece were deployed along a defensive line that could be outflanked by an opponent moving simply through Yugoslav territory. This nation of disparate groups was split in its sympathies and was under heavy diplomatic pressure from Germany to join the Axis. Owing to their poor equipment, both Yugoslavia and Turkey were perceived by the British as liabilities rather than assets, but Churchill was convinced of their need to remain resolute. On 25 March Yugoslavia's predominantly Serbian cabinet yielded to demands and signed a so-called Tripartite Pact with the Axis. This resulted, two days later, in a *coup d'état* by forces loyal to the under-age King. While the nation still did not declare for the Allied cause, Hitler was enraged at events. Despite the obvious effect that it would have on the tight schedule for 'Barbarossa', he resolved to take Belgrade as part of a larger plan to occupy the Greek province of Thrace. The relentless German military build-up, from the Baltic coast to Romania, could not be disguised and was the subject of numerous warnings to Stalin. To these the dictator closed his ears, for reasons which have never been fully explained.

By the end of March 1941 over 40,000 British and Commonwealth personnel, their equipment and supplies, had been ferried to Greece. Admiral Cunningham, quietly echoed by the CIGS, was convinced of its political correctness but had 'grave uncertainty of its military expedience'. So concerned was he that, even before 'Lustre' was complete, he had his staff commence planning means of pulling the two divisions out again. Primitive Greek airfields and an insufficiency of resources saw the Royal Air Force unable to offer more than a limited cover, with the result that 'Lustre' cost the destruction of 25 valuable merchantmen, almost all to *Luftwaffe* aircraft working out of the Dodecanese. The Prime Minister, nonetheless, remained enthusiastic. British successes in North Africa and at Matapan, then the Yugoslav *coup d'état*, convinced him that the Greek operation had been transfigured from a 'military adventure dictated by *noblesse oblige* [into] a prime mover in the larger design'.

Early on 6 April Germany declared war on both Greece and Yugoslavia. Not only was Belgrade bombed to the tune of 17,000 deaths, but a raid on the port of Piraeus succeeded in blowing up the ammunition-laden cargo liner *Clan Fraser*, devastating one of the country's few major facilities and destroying a further 42,000grt of shipping. Advancing as forecast through Yugoslavia, the German armies forced its military to seek an armistice on 14 April, while causing an almost continuous retreat to the British. On the 19th Wavell flew to Athens to discuss withdrawal at the highest level. For a while it appeared that Churchill's overdeveloped sense of history would cause the British to make a disastrous stand on the ancient field of Thermopylae, but the Greek capitulation on 24 April scotched his plan.

The Royal Navy, having carried out Operation 'Lustre' and supported it by seven weeks' worth of supply convoys, now found itself required to throw everything into reverse. This operation, coded 'Demon', depended greatly upon Vice-Admiral Pridham-Wippell's cruisers and destroyers, based on Suda Bay. Although Crete was only some sixty miles from the Greek mainland at its closest point, the primitive nature of the island meant that the distance between the locations suitable for the operation could easily triple this. Experience at Dunkirk highlighted the need for a large number of small craft capable of shuttling between the shore and the ships anchored off. The vital role of naval liaison officer ashore was shouldered by Rear Admiral Baillie-Grohman. The crew of *York* abandoned attempts to salvage their ship and were drafted *en masse* to form beach parties or to man requisitioned small craft.

With the *Luftwaffe* now virtually unopposed, ships could arrive only one hour after dark, load and be away by 0300 if they were to be beyond easy Stuka range by daylight. Another Dunkirk loomed in terms of equipment as Army personnel could bring only personal weapons and kit, together with small, valuable items such as gunnery optics. What was useful to the Greek population (but not the enemy) could be handed over and the rest destroyed or despoiled. Some 8,000 vehicles, badly needed in North Africa, were lost. It had been the intention to ferry troops by shuttle service to Crete, whence convoys would take them to Alexandria. There was a dearth of suitable trans-shipment points on the island, however, and troop transports were soon brought direct to Greece to supplement the capacity of the warships. This arrangement inevitably slowed pro-ceedings.

Five Greek beaches were identified as suitable both for small-craft operation and for larger ships to lay off. During the first night of 'Demon', 24/25 April, nearly 6,000 New Zealanders were lifted from Porto Raphti (about twelve miles from Athens) and 7,000 British from Nauplia in the Peloponnesus. An early casualty at the latter location was *Ulster Prince*. Small and fast, cross-channellers such as she were particularly valuable, but she ran aground attempting to enter the port and was bombed to destruction.

Again *Hotspur* was deeply involved. As her First Lieutenant recalled, 'Dunkirk had given us good experience of this . . . The guns' crews had been splicing special slings with which to hoist army stretchers from a rocking boat, and noosed recovery lines for hauling men out of the water. "Cooky" had been baking a double load of bread, and all the supply and canteen staff were making up giant sandwiches and preparing fannies full of cocoa . . . some of the upper mess deck was roped off for operations. If a leg had to come off, then a mess table was the best place to do it . . .'

This destroyer was one of the escorts to a pair of passenger ships, *Slamat* and *Khedive Ismail*. Loading proceeded very slowly and, still less than full, the group sailed at 0415. Daylight brought the Stukas and Ju 88s. The old anti-aircraft cruiser *Calcutta* placed herself between the transports to lend maximum protection, but the armament of the destroyers was essentially low-angle and of little use. A clutch of four bombs turned the Dutch *Slamat* into an instant fiery ruin. The destroyers *Diamond* and *Wryneck* went alongside and removed all survivors. Grossly overloaded, they succumbed to later bombing and strafing: only fifty men survived from the three ships. On 26 April German paratroops seized the line of the Corinth Canal, effectively isolating the Peloponnesus. Of 7,000 rear-echelon personnel stranded at Kalamata, only a few hundred could be rescued by destroyers using small boats over an open beach.

Generally, 'Demon' was a success in that it rescued 51,000 personnel, or over 80 per cent of those involved. The last, official, return run was made to the fabled island of Milos during the night of 30 April/1 May. The perspective 'from the other side of the hill' is interesting. Where 'Demon' was considered by the British to be a touch-and-go undertaking, Rommel quoted it, alongside Dunkirk and Åndalsnes, as evidence that a British army could never be trapped in large numbers as long as it had access to the sea. He considered it a mistake for Germany to become embroiled in Greece, the aircraft so committed being of greater value in the protection of Axis convoys to North Africa. In his view, had Malta been taken instead, the whole British stand in the Mediterranean would have collapsed under a 'domino effect'.

A visit to Rommel's front by General Hoffman von Waldau, Deputy to the *Luftwaffe* Chief of Staff, produced a highly pessimistic report on the Axis supply situation, including an unwarranted implication that the Italians were not doing their utmost at the convoy end of the logistics line. Gring's response was immediate and reassuring. Extra *Luftwaffe* assets would be transferred to step up the pressure on Malta, the Suez Canal and the Royal Navy in general. With the Greek campaign reaching a successful conclusion, a large and battle-hardened force, with high morale, would shortly be available to seize the island. However, at a point when Malta's future looked most precarious, Hitler's attention was diverted by Crete. This island had been the means by which a British withdrawal from Greece had not degenerated into a rout. Its situation would enable the *Luftwaffe* to range over the eastern basin, dominating the

Delta, without bothering with Malta, which would become an irrelevance. It could be taken by German forces alone—a further indication of the poor standard of relations between the Axis partners. Despite protest, the *Führer* insisted.

Where the Italian Navy was deficient was in the challenging of British sea control. Its general lack of aggression and initiative comes through in its every assessment. Cunningham could take no positive action with the Mediterranean Fleet at this stage because all its escorts were committed to 'Demon'. That all convoys from Crete to Alexandria ran without loss is a painful demonstration of the Italian Navy's lack of offensive spirit.

Churchill's readiness to support Greece and his vision of a united Balkans front generated much popular sympathy in the United States, whose wider assistance he was actively wooing. Without doubt the Prime Minister heaped too great a load of responsibility on to General Wavell, an immediate consequence of which was that the defence of Crete did not get the attention that it deserved. The area around Suda Bay benefited from the arrival of the Royal Marines' Mobile Naval Base Defence Organization (MNBDO), but this was just one location in a mountainous and undeveloped island about 160 miles in length. There had been half a dozen changes of military command on Crete in as many months and, when asked to rule on priorities on 18 April, London had placed the defence of the island behind victory in Libya, evacuation from Greece and support for Tobruk. General Wavell flew to Crete on 30 April, found 'considerable confusion' and selected the New Zealand Maj-Gen Freyberg VC for overall command. His aerial defence was almost non-existent and his military resources totally insufficient to secure the island's long and desolate coastline.

Throughout April the force of Ju 52 transport aircraft on Romanian and Bulgarian airfields had steadily expanded, but British awareness of an interest in Crete was slow to materialize. German intentions were made clear in 'Ultra' decrypts only on 25 April; on the 30th a German instruction not to mine Suda Bay nor to bomb Cretan airfields confirmed matters. General Freyberg organized his defence around four self-contained pockets on the island's north coast and, while shipping was yet available, sent as many non-combatants as possible back to Alexandria. He had, nonetheless, to depend on a mix of battle-weary Anzacs and some 14,000 'untrained and unarmed' Greeks. Also on the island were a similar number of Italian prisoners of war. 'Ultra' confirmed that the initial assault would be from the air, a massive effort to seize three key airfields, following which convoys would arrive with heavy equipment and further troops. In all, 1,300 aircraft and 30,000 troops would be involved, under the command of General Student, who had used airborne forces with spectacular success in the Low Countries the year previously.

Freyberg felt confident about defeating an aerial assault but, with so much unguarded coastline, feared a landing over the beach. Cunningham well recognized his concern, making the repulse of any landing groups his first priority. His own problem was one of air cover for the Fleet, *Formidable*'s air wing having been reduced to precisely four aircraft. There were shortfalls in every aspect of air cover, and the C-in-C was obliged to plan on the basis of sweeping the area and its approaches by night and withdrawing to the relative safety of the open sea by day. The Mediterranean Fleet was organized to maintain a standing battleship patrol to the west of Crete, to meet any incursion on the part of the Italian Navy, and to form three cruiser/destroyer task groups to tackle enemy assault convoys. To co-operate more closely with his fellow service chiefs, Admiral Cunningham remained in Alexandria.

Because the British knew so much about the German plan (Operation 'Merkur'), naval dispositions were made in good time, only to be caught out by a need to refuel when the enemy unexpectedly had to delay matters by 72 hours. Nonetheless, when proceedings commenced early on 20 May, two battleships (*Warspite*, with Rear-Admiral H. B. Rawlings, and *Valiant*) were on station while a pair of cruiser groups were pulling out on their daytime dispositions.

Two hours of sustained bombing 'softened up' the defences before 53 gliders arrived with a battalion of assault troops. Their task was to secure the selected drop zones, but they incurred crippling casualties from the mainly New Zealand defenders. Almost oblivious to losses (one battalion alone lost 400 dead out of an establishment of 600), paratroops poured down. Many Germans could not find or reach their weapon containers and the few available British tanks were able to wreak havoc.

By the day's end the key airfields were still in British hands but the remnants of the Royal Air Force (just four Hurricanes and three Gladiators) had been withdrawn. Now, perhaps, would have been an appropriate time to demolish runways, but the defenders held on in anticipation of success. Slowly, the enemy's numbers grew, while the defenders' resources shrank almost without replacement.

In an effort to reduce hostile air activity, Captain Mack's destroyers bombarded the airfield on Scarpanto during the night of 20/21 May. The ships had to beat off an attack by Italian MAS boats, while the shelling was akin to poking a wasps' nest with a stick to look for signs of life. Dawn brought sustained high-level bombing, which sank the destroyer *Juno* and damaged the supporting cruiser *Ajax*.

By the second day of the battle, 21 May, the key airfield at Maleme, littered with the wrecks of eighty crashed Ju 52s, passed into German hands. Behind schedule and surprised by the ferocity of the defence, Student requested that the follow-up convoys from Piraeus be sailed early.

That for Suda Bay comprised a motley collection of fishing craft and local caiques crammed with nearly 2,500 troops and Italian marines of the San Marco regiment. Their sole escort was the torpedo boat *Lupo*.

The convoy's progress was accurately charted and, when almost at its destination, was attacked that night by a task group under Rear-Admiral Glennie. If anything, the British were present in too large a number, and always had to waste valuable time in challenging before firing. Thus *Lupo*, though hit a reported eighteen times by shells that passed through her light structure without exploding, survived. Ten of her charges were destroyed and, though casualties to troops could be numbered in hundreds rather than in the thousands claimed at the time, the action (clearly in view of the defenders ashore) caused a great fillip to morale.

Glennie's action greatly depleted his dual-purpose ammunition and, though he was under orders to stand-on and rendezvous with a second group under Rear-Admiral King, he judged that his ships would be a liability in the event of air attack and he decided to withdraw to the south. King had duly intercepted an even larger, but equally poorly protected, convoy. This had, on order, already reversed course, but now 4,000 troops were at the mercy of four cruisers and three destroyers. It should have resulted in annihilation, but King was a worried man. His high-angle ammunition was already low, machinery problems on the elderly *Carlisle* confined his force to less than 21kts and, at 0830 on a fine morning, he was deep in enemy territory. Nonetheless, killing enemy troops was clearly what Admiral Cunningham had meant by the 'Navy's first priority'. King would have been justified in risking the loss of his entire force to achieve success, but he allowed himself to be unnerved by combination air attacks and a courageous stand by the lone escort, *Sagittario*.

Only a few caiques had been destroyed when, to the enemy's disbelief, the British pulled out to the south-west. Cunningham's subsequent criticism was a model of restraint, but Churchill's was scathing. The only ameliorating factor was that the convoy returned to Greece and, if its cargo ever landed on Crete, the die was already cast.

Rear-Admiral Rawlings, commanding the main fleet, steered to meet King, two of whose cruisers had, by now, been damaged by bombing; once combined, the group came under the command of King, the senior officer. The destroyer *Greyhound* was detached to sink a single caique, reported in the Kithera Channel. Returning, she was jumped by Stukas, which sank her with two hits. King immediately dispatched the destroyers *Kandahar* and *Kingston* to rescue survivors, these ships being covered by the cruisers *Gloucester* and *Fiji*. These had signalled already that their high-angle ammunition had been reduced to 18 and 30 per cent respectively. They soon came under heavy aerial attack and King authorized them to withdraw at their own discretion.

It was too late. By 1550, her decks a shambles, *Gloucester* came to a halt, from the effects of several hits. *Fiji* had already been reduced to firing inert practice projectiles and could not stay. Jettisoning her rafts for *Gloucester*'s benefit, she grimly kept going. Over 700 went down with *Gloucester*, the survivors, as so often in this savage campaign, being mercilessly machine-gunned as they were in the water. *Fiji* survived over twenty separate attacks and looked set to escape when, at 1845, a single fighter-bomber narrowly missed her with a 250kg bomb. Not for the first time, the mining effect of a near-miss proved more devastating than an actual hit. Dead in the water and devoid of ammunition, she fell easy prey to a second such attack. Over 500 of her men were eventually rescued by the two destroyers.

Although the Royal Navy was suffering, its continued activities greatly concerned the enemy, for the battle ashore remained in the balance and there was an urgent need to ship-in heavy equipment. An intercepted order for a major *Luftwaffe* effort against the Fleet was, therefore, not unexpected, but there was little that anybody could do except carry on as before. Sweeps and bombardments during the night of 22/23 May kept the remaining three destroyers of Mountbatten's 5th Flotilla overlong in Cretan waters. At 0800 they were heavily attacked by two dozen Stukas. As Admiral Rawlings' priority at this time was to cover the destroyers *Decoy* and *Hero*, which were evacuating the King of Greece and the British Ambassador, Mountbatten was unsupported and lost both his own ship, *Kelly*, and *Kashmir*. The remaining ship, *Kipling*, made Alexandria safely bearing 279 survivors. At the same time, the LSI *Glenroy* was approaching the island with a battalion embarked. Cunningham knew that she would not survive the day and, having consulted General Wavell, recalled her at about 1130 on the 23rd. London disagreed, insisting at 1600 that the ship be turned back towards Crete. The C-in-C angrily reminded the Admiralty that the ship could thus arrive only in daylight, when her destruction would be certain. Quite unnecessarily, London reminded Cunningham that the loss of Crete would have serious repercussions, but the Admiral won the day.

In a report to the Chiefs of Staff, Cunningham stated that his ships, in current circumstances, could not operate by day off Crete or in the Aegean. He could no longer guarantee to prevent a seaborne landing without incurring losses on a scale that would prejudice his ability to control the eastern basin. At a time when scores of Ju 52s were operating an almost unhindered shuttle service through the key airfield at Maleme, the C-in-Cs were told by the Chiefs of Staff that 'any risk' was to be accepted by both the Fleet and the Royal Air Force.

The main threat came from Stuka dive-bombers, so Cunningham was obliged to risk his solitary carrier, *Formidable*, in a strike against their main base on Scarpanto. So few aircraft remained serviceable to her that the raid, at 0500 on the 26th, was undertaken by just four Albacores and five Fulmars. This pinprick inevitably attracted a full-scale riposte, during which the carrier suffered two hits by 500kg bombs. The damage was such that the ship had to be sent to the United States for repair. Her resulting removal from the Order of Battle for over six months was, as the C-in-C had forecast, a disastrous return for an operation that could never have offered a commensurate gain.

On this same day, the 26th, General Freyberg reported to Wavell that Crete could not be held. If a withdrawal were planned and executed promptly, then at least some personnel could be rescued. The alternative was to lose both island and personnel. Freyberg's courage and record were legendary but, even so, the Prime Minister tried to avert a decision by rhetoric. Wavell had wearily to remind him that this was simply not enough—the New Zealand general was in earnest. By 27 May it was reported that, with the surrounding area now being overrun, Suda Bay itself would be untenable within twenty-four hours. Plans were therefore formulated quickly to march troops across the grain of the mountainous island and to evacuate some 23,000 personnel through the tiny fishing port of Sphakia.

Area by area, Freyberg's defensive enclaves dissolved, the survivors making their way as best they could to the south coast, buoyed by the belief that the Navy would be there. Though the latter succeeded completely in preventing a seaborne invasion of Crete, its first priority, the island was lost anyway. Bruised and bloodied, the Mediterranean Fleet steadied itself for a further opposed emergency evacuation. There was no way that it could let the Army down. In the event, between 4,000 and 4,500 troops defending Heraklion, on the north coast, would need to be evacuated from there to avoid being cut off, while the number from the Sphakia area appeared to be about 15,000.

Rear-Admiral Rawlings decided boldly to take three cruisers and six destroyers to Heraklion and lift the garrison in one operation. All present realized fully that the location of the port would entail a good bombing in each direction. From 1730 until the onset of darkness at about 2100 the guns' crews worked without respite. No ship was hit but several were heavily concussed, including the long-suffering *Ajax*, which turned back after dark.

Destroyers could just berth in pairs alongside Heraklion mole and, in total silence, they collected their loads, in sequence moving out to decant them into the waiting cruisers. By 0320 the job was complete and the formation heading east at maximum speed. The badly shaken destroyer *Imperial* then suffered a major mechanical breakdown and, to avoid further delay, was sunk by torpedo. Detailed for the task was *Hotspur* which, now with 900 people aboard and mindful of *Diamond*'s fate, made off flat-out after the main body.

Selflessly, Rawlings waited farther down the coast, but the extra delay was to prove expensive. Sustained bombing first claimed the destroyer *Hereward*, then, untroubled by any aerial escort, the Stukas concentrated on the cruisers. Both *Dido* and *Orion* had turrets demolished by direct hits, the latter also taking a bomb which penetrated to the crowded mess-decks before exploding. Of 1,100 troops aboard, a quarter were killed and a quarter injured. Her Captain dead and the Admiral wounded, and with her fuel tanks ruptured and contaminated by sea water, *Orion* staggered home, steering with her engines and followed by a fluctuating pall of multi-hued smoke. During the same night, four large destroyers offloaded urgently needed ammunition at Sphakia beach, returning unscathed with 700 troops. One of the period's unsolved mysteries is why *Supermarina* did not commit the Italian Fleet totally to hit the Royal Navy at the time of its greatest trial and while it was operating in an unavoidably fragmented fashion.

A now-concerned Admiralty asked of Cunningham whether further evacuation could justify the losses in warships. The Admiral's response was memorable: 'It takes the Navy three years to build a new ship. It will take three hundred years to build a new tradition. The evacuation will continue'. During the night of 29/30 May a major effort lifted over 6,000 men between 1130 and 0315. The key to this were LCAs (Assault Landing Craft), carried there by the LSI *Glengyle*. These were left on site and enabled destroyers to embark a further 1,400 the next night. A few Royal Air Force fighters, fitted with long-range tanks, gave what cover they could and, during the early hours of the 31st, a special effort was made to take off as many of the rearguard as possible. Only five ships were serviceable, but in less than four hours of furious activity they again lifted nearly 4,000. It was grossly unfortunate that many of the Royal Marines and Commonwealth troops that fought to the end to cover the evacuation of their comrades had to be abandoned to surrender.

In all, some 16,500 troops were evacuated. The ten-day campaign had cost about 15,300 killed, wounded or captured. Two thousand of these were Royal Navy personnel, of which a high proportion—40 per cent—were fatalities. Three cruisers and six destroyers had been lost and sixteen other ships considerably damaged. As off Norway, an unopposed *Luftwaffe* had proved all too effective.

Viewed objectively, the loss of Crete was not entirely a bad thing. Over six thousand of Germany's paratroop élite had been lost in a Pyrrhic victory that immediately reduced the threat to the strategically more important Malta—though few realized it at the time. About 220 German aircraft had been lost and 150 damaged. The Royal Navy no longer needed to support and supply the island. The Germans, once in possession, were to make little more use of the island than had the British before them. Nevertheless, despite Great Britain's honourable enough motives in involving herself in Greece, the campaign was yet another improvisation that cost much in material and prestige. A still-neutral United States criticized British war policy and Greece herself was to endure dark years of occupation, being punished both for humiliating Mussolini and for defying Hitler.

Troubles, of course, never come singly, and General Wavell, at the same time as dealing with Crete and the Western Desert, had the responsibility of providing the forces to put down Rashid Ali's pro-German insurrection in Iraq (thus safeguarding a considerable source of oil) and to take over Syria, where indications were that the Vichy French occupation forces were to move out in favour of Germans. This information was, in fact, less than accurate, and tetchy exchanges between Wavell and Churchill are indicative of how grossly overloaded the General had become.

The force used to take Syria was predominantly Australian and Indian, with Free French representation. Necessarily, the campaign was rather *ad hoc*, but it was no pushover, the Vichy military forces often fighting tenaciously, with air cover in superior strength. Also present were French naval units that could not be ignored. In Beirut there were two 'super-destroyers' (*Guépard* and *Valmy*) together with three submarines. On the coast were Vice-Admiral King's flagship, *Phoebe*, the ubiquitous *Ajax* and a scattered force of ten destroyers. These were initially forbidden to fire on the French but, when the latter slipped out to bombard forward Australian positions, things changed.

Having let go sixty rounds, the French headed back to the north, only to run into a dispersed group of four British destroyers. Though a decade older, the French ships had twice the displacement of the British units, several knots' advantage in speed and, importantly, five 138mm (5.45in) guns apiece. The British were considerably embarrassed when the French not only chose to fight but also to do so from the answerable range of 17,000yds (15,500m). The leader, *Janus*, was heavily hit by five shells and brought to a halt, whereupon she was covered by her sister, *Jackal*, which laid smoke. Keeping the range to a minimum of 11,000yds (10,000m), the French satisfied honour and loped back to Beirut with the two older British ships, *Hotspur* and *Isis*, puffing along behind. All survived the day, but it could have gone badly.

On the same day, *Ajax* was narrowly missed by a torpedo from the French submarine *Caiman*. As the Royal Air Force was too stretched to provide fighter cover, FAA Fulmars flew from bases in Palestine, but they were badly outclassed by the French opposition. Ships now being in very short supply, the Royal Air Force had to be redirected to support them rather than troops ashore. Despite this measure, the destroyer *Isis* was damaged by German aircraft and her sister, *Ilex*, by French.

Short of ammunition, the Vichy authorities ran a cargo in the 'super-destroyer' *Chevalier Paul*, only to have her sunk on the night of 16/17 June by FAA Swordfish working from Cyprus. The French tried again with *Vauquelin*. She reached Beirut but, with the tanker *Adour*, which held the entire French bunker fuel stock, was torpedoed and badly damaged at anchor. Admiral Cunningham moved up the New Zealand cruiser *Leander* and the Australian destroyer *Stuart*. These succeeded in waylaying *Guépard* but, though winged by a 6in shell, the latter used her 38kt speed to escape. German 'Enigma' keys were being used by the Vichy French at this time, which probably accounts for the success of Albacores catching a further ammunition shipment when the merchantman *Saint-Didier* was sunk off the Turkish coast. A French submarine, *Souffleur*, was torpedoed and sunk by the British submarine *Parthian* near Junieh.

On 11 July 1941 the French in Syria capitulated, arrangements having to be agreed to give free passage for 21 passenger liners carrying 34,000 repatriates. This bitter little campaign had cost about 5,000 casualties to either side, but it had demonstrated Allied resolve to Turkey, Syria's northern neighbour. Securing the Levant and Iraq isolated Persia (Iran) from direct Axis influence. This state was not only a further prolific oil source but was also along the shortest route to supply the Soviet Union, which, once 'Barbarossa' broke on 22 June, became aligned with the Allied camp. About 3,000 Germans were employed in Persia, many in influential posts, and this fact was used as pretext to take the country after a short struggle. It was a shabby business, described later by Churchill as a 'brief and fruitful exercise in overwhelming force against a weak and ancient state'.

In retrospect, General Wavell's responsibilities in April and May appear too much for any one person to shoulder—Greece, Crete, Iraq, the Western Desert, six separate territories in East Africa and, coming up, Syria, and Persia. No 'thin red line' was ever stretched more thinly.

SIX

The 'Dominant Theatre'

May 1941 to July 1941

HITLER'S DECISION to accord the capture of Crete a higher priority than that of Malta was received by his headquarters staff with less than unanimous approval. *Oberstgeneral* Alfred Jodl, Chief of *Wehrmacht* Operations, knew of the imminence of 'Barbarossa' and its enormous potential demands on *Luftwaffe* resources. Such air power as then remained in the Mediterranean theatre would have the support of the *Afrika Korps* (DAK) as its main priority. With the weight of aerial assault on it thus lifted, Malta would be reinforced immediately so that the convoy routes could be ravaged.

Not that *Fliegerkorps X* had been getting things all its own way. In each of April and May it had mounted nearly 400 bombing sorties, but at the cost of almost 100 aircraft, mostly the versatile Ju 88. The mounting losses of experienced air crews led to a dilution and a marked drop in aggressiveness and efficiency. So obvious was this trend that the Deputy *Luftwaffe* Chief of Staff, General Hoffmann von Waldau, suggested that operations be suspended for a period of re-equipment and re-training.

Reichsmarschall Göring's response was to redefine the formation's duties. About 150 aircraft would remain in North Africa and 240 be transferred from Sicily to Greece, whence they would operate against the Royal Navy, the Delta and the Canal. They would also cover a new proposed convoy route, running from Taranto/Brindisi coastwise to the Greek capes and thence to Benghazi. Shipping on this track would be under continuous cover from land-based air, while being further removed from Malta's strike forces.

The weakness of the plan lay in the High Command's willingness to believe that Malta could be subdued indefinitely by the Italian Air Force. Protestations to this effect were, however, ignored, and within a month *Fliegerkorps X* had been withdrawn from the theatre. The reduction in aerial activity over Malta was at once evident, with blessed relief to the Dockyard in particular. Minelaying had been a problem, the destroyer *Jersey* being sunk just beyond the breakwater on 2 May. A week later, four 'Flowers', equipped for minesweeping, arrived. As the lone *Gloxinia* led the Malta element of the 'Tiger' convoy into Grand Harbour, she set off a dozen explosions.

Despite the loss of *Usk* in May 1941, Captain Simpson's 10th Submarine Flotilla was increasing in strength, which varied between five and ten 'U' class boats and an occasional 'T', usually destined for the Alexandria-based 1st Flotilla. During February, Lt E. D. Norman, in *Upright*, fired at a couple of shapes that nearly ran him down on a moonless night near Lampedusa. He rather modestly claimed a hit on a target 'bigger than destroyers'. The loss of the light cruiser *Armando Diaz* became known a few days later.

Another of Simpson's boats was *Upholder*, whose skipper, Lt. M. D. Wanklyn, began so indifferently that his Captain wondered how anybody 'whose torpedo expenditure [was] without result . . . could be kept in command'. Simpson's tolerance was to be amply rewarded.

A third flotilla, the understrength 8th, was based at Gibraltar. Two of its units were the large 'fleet' boats *Clyde* and *Severn*, employed in the carriage of stores and personnel to and from Malta. A large submarine could, routinely, stow about 12–15 tons, but *Clyde*, at the expense of one-third of her battery capacity, had been modified to accept about 120 tons. One load could keep Malta in fuel, for instance, for three days. Also serving with the 8th Flotilla were three Dutch 'O' boats. A fourth had already been sunk in Norwegian waters, but the rest went on to destroy a credited 21 enemy ships of about 66,300 gross tons and the German *U95*.

Having delivered her cargo to Malta, the large minelaying submarine *Cachalot* patrolled offensively, as was customary, on the return leg. In poor visibility she surfaced to sink a merchantman by gunfire, only to discover that her quarry was, in fact, an elderly torpedo boat, which promptly holed her pressure hull with a shot. Unable to dive, she was sunk after the Italians allowed the crew to leave.

Italian topography is generally such that road and rail hug the coast, affording great opportunities to submarine skippers of sporting inclination. So popular did the landing of demolition parties and the shelling of transport become that Simpson argued that, for 'negligible effort', he was tying down an estimated 2,500 Italian troops in futile deterrence. Inevitably a convoy was missed, and the Captain was curtly reminded of his primary targets. Italian State Railways again began to run to time.

With the tempo of *Luftwaffe* raids slackening and the appointment of a new and energetic AOC, Air Vice-Marshal Hugh Lloyd, Malta's strike potential improved measurably. During April and May the Royal Navy's carriers flew off over 100 fighters for the island, but these were boosted by a further 150 in June alone.

The 'Tiger' convoy arrived at Alexandria on 12 May, and General Wavell, already deeply committed in Crete, began to be pushed hard by a

Prime Minister anxious to see the operation which would use the armour thus delivered. Wavell had issued preliminary instructions for this, Operation 'Battleaxe', in early May but his intentions were well read by the intuitively good military sense of Rommel. The latter expected particularly that there would be a thrust to relieve Tobruk, whose support was known to be a major drain on the Royal Navy's resources. Rommel, in odium with his High Command for grossly exceeding his brief, could, in any case, advance no further, so he dug in thoroughly, with minefields covered by artillery. Wavell, prey to doubts regarding the quality of British equipment, showed little sense of urgency and was subjected to Churchill's wrath. This was vented also upon the long-suffering Air Marshal Longmore, whose reasonable criticisms of London's performance finally saw him called home, on 1 June, 'for consultations'. His absence was the opportunity to replace him with his deputy, Air Marshal A. T. Tedder.

'Battleaxe' opened on 15 June, 1941 and involved two understrength divisions on either side. Wavell's objectives were comparatively modest, pushing columns westwards to take, first, both ends of the strategically important Haifaya Pass, then the border area in the triangle Sollum–Capuzzo–Bardia. The DAK was holding Halfaya in strength and placed most of its mobile forces as a fluid reserve, the majority just north of Capuzzo.

Tedder covered the British approach well by drawing aircraft from every conceivable location. Unfortunately the slow but highly robust British 'I' tanks ran into a combination of minefields and 88mm guns and the attack at Halfaya stagnated. Further west, Capuzzo was taken by armoured forces but, on the Hafid Ridge, British tanks again suffered heavily at the hands of well-sited artillery. Poor communications made for equally poor co-operation among British armour, infantry and artillery, so that Rommel, though under pressure, suffered far fewer casualties in tanks, particularly as he retained possession of the field. Intercepted British radio communications also betrayed an intention to seek a decisive armour-on-armour clash. German doctrine, however, was to use armoured vehicles to open up weak points in an enemy line, not to fight other tanks: this was a job for artillery, suitably sited and supported.

On the second day the British enjoyed considerable success when the DAK attacked a combination of dug-in 'I' tanks and 25pdr guns, but any advantage was thrown away elsewhere when cruiser tanks, being used like cavalry, outran the support of their artillery and were badly cut about.

Still aware that the British were holding the bulk of their armour in the hope of a decisive attack, Rommel decided on an abrupt shift in the battle's centre of gravity. Before first light on the 17th his armour streamed eastwards, with a primary aim of relieving the forces holding out at Halfaya. The British had already lost heavily in armour without ever meeting Rommel's main strength and now, as they looked increasingly like being marooned too far to the west, they began an eastward retirement. 'Battleaxe' was effectively over.

Both sides learned much. Rommel berated his subordinate commanders for not acting sufficiently on their initiative to capitalize on British mistakes and a full knowledge of British intentions. Wavell took the blame for the failure, but all understood that he had allowed himself to be hustled by the Prime Minister into a premature offensive. Churchill, having run the risks of shipping the armour the length of the Mediterranean in the 'Tiger' convoy, was now bitterly disappointed to learn that, of 90 cruiser tanks, 27 had been lost, together with two-thirds of the heavy 'I' tanks. Wavell's reward was to exchange appointments with General Sir Claude Auchinleck, C-in-C India. In tacit acknowledgement that Wavell's task had been impossible, Auchinleck was assisted by the creation of two new local posts, an 'Intendant-General', to supervise administration, and a Minister of State in the Middle East, to handle the many political ramifications of a theatre that was very widely spread.

While finding that Auchinleck was to be no pushover, Churchill immediately began pressing for a new offensive (Operation 'Crusader'), to begin early in November 1941. For this, the new C-in-C chose Lt-Gen Alan Cunningham, brother to the naval C-in-C, as tactical commander. For the moment Rommel had stretched his logistics line to the utmost and could go no further. For their part, the British still did not appreciate that the Germans had no intention of indulging in large-scale tank-to-tank combat. The British also had the impression that German tanks were better armed and armoured than was, in fact, the case. It was still not realized that a large proportion of losses had been caused by a few well-sited 88mm guns. The role of these weapons in low-angle support had been documented since the Spanish Civil War, yet their effectiveness still came as a surprise to many.

The launch of 'Barbarossa' in June 1941 had repercussions in the Mediterranean theatre. First, if the Soviets crumbled before the onslaught, the way lay open for German advance, southwards between the Caspian and Black Seas to threaten the whole oil-producing area of the Middle East. Second, so much had been committed to the German offensive that little would be left with which to counter a British thrust in the Western Desert. London envisaged the recapture of Cyrenaica and the relief of Tobruk and, with the latter, a reduction in demands made on the Royal Navy. Neither Auchinleck nor Tedder, however, would agree to advancing the 'Crusader' timetable, and both won promises of substantial reinforcements.

Early in June, Hitler and Mussolini, and their Chiefs of Staff, Keitel and Cavellero, had held discussions at the Brenner Pass. While the Germans recognized that the war in North Africa was 'a problem of logistics and equipment, not of mass concentrations', the final advance on the Delta, even as the Prime Minister had feared, would be a double thrust from the Western Desert and through Iraq. Such an operation would have to await the outcome of 'Barbarossa' and the release of forces, but Admiral Raeder could not agree to such a precondition: the campaign in Greece and Crete had created a momentum which should be maintained. He proposed a continuation of heavy pressure through the utilization of Italian forces under German control. This contentious idea was based on his low opinion of Italian training and leadership, tempered by his experience of Italians performing well with German planning, organization and discipline.

Raeder listed the constituent parts of a successful offensive: heavy bombing of the British Fleet and a concentration of submarine activity against it; a heavy programme of mining, utilizing the Italian surface fleet to close off the Central Narrows completely; and the taking of Malta and Tobruk quickly as possible. The Admiral referred also to the growing tide of American aid which, in the long term, would be decisive if action were not taken first. His case, while sound, went unheeded as his *Führer*'s gaze was set firmly eastwards.

Relationships between the Axis partners remained confused. Even before the outset of 'Barbarossa', Mussolini had an Army Corps and 200 front-line aircraft earmarked to assist. In vain did the Germans point out that these aircraft were needed in North Africa, and only in North Africa, and they were deployed to Romania in August. To keep closer control on events, the Germans had Maj-Gen Alfred Gause posted to Gariboldi's headquarters. Alarmed, the Italians promptly replaced Gariboldi with General Bastico, seen as more able to keep their ally in his place.

Not to be outdone, the German High Command upgraded their military force to 'Panzer Group Africa', with *Panzergeneral* Rommel in command and Gause as his Chief of Staff. Tactical command was the responsibility of Lt-Gen Ludwig Cruewell, with two panzer divisions (250 tanks) and a motorized division. In addition, the Italians had one armoured, one motorized and four infantry divisions. Supporting this considerable force, the Italian convoy system was delivering an average of over 90,000 tons per month, more than sufficient for routine consumption. Even Rommel, however, seemed unable to appreciate fully that shortages at the front could be ascribed almost entirely to the limitations in his overland supply route. Should the British remain quiescent, he aimed to reduce the Tobruk garrison before the end of the year and move on into Egypt in February 1942.

Not aware of the true extent of German casualties in Crete, the British assumed that the successful assault here would soon be followed by a similar descent on Malta. The Governor, Lt-Gen Dobbie, was granted substantial reinforcement and, with the Axis now firmly dominating the Crete–Cyrenaica gap, this would need to be run from the Gibraltar end. In preparation, Force 'H' ran a pair of sorties in late June, the carriers *Ark Royal* and *Furious* flying-in 57 Hurricanes. The convoy itself, code-named 'Substance', comprised six fast cargo liners and a single cross-channeller with personnel reinforcement. As two of the Italian battleships damaged at Taranto were thought to be again operational, it was deemed advisable to beef up the escort with a contingent from the Home Fleet, whose responsibilities had been lightened somewhat by the recent demise of the German battleship *Bismarck*.

An initial move was for Admiral Cunningham to sail in strength from Alexandria, to engage the Italians' attention. Spoof signal traffic would be generated from two submarines, sited west of Crete, to increase the tension. During the night of 20/21 July 1941 the 'Substance' convoy swept eastwards past Gibraltar, accompanied by the reassuring bulk of the battleship *Nelson*, three cruisers (*Arethusa*, *Edinburgh* and *Manchester*) and five fleet destroyers. To add extra anti-aircraft protection with their 4in high-angle armaments were three 'Hunt' class escort destroyers and the fast minelayer *Manxman*, one of the class that proved so generally valuable in the Mediterranean.

Fog in the Strait concealed the movement but resulted in the personnel carrier *Leinster* running aground. Admiral Somerville sailed with Force 'H' but kept clear of the convoy as his departure would certainly have been reported. The precaution paid off, for Italian reconnaissance sighted him south of the Balearics the following day, without the existence of 'Substance' yet being suspected. As Somerville had *Ark Royal* in company, it was assumed that he was ferrying yet more fighters to Malta.

Not until the 23rd was the convoy discovered, south of Sardinia, whereupon a skilful air attack developed. High-level bombing lured *Ark Royal*'s Fulmars to altitude, then six torpedo bombers swept in at wave height. They achieved two hits. One badly slowed *Manchester*, which had to turn back. The other disabled the destroyer *Fearless*, which, blazing, was finished by a further torpedo from her sister *Forester* once survivors had been removed. Further air attacks were frustrated by carrier-based fighters, and at 1700, as planned, Force 'H' and *Nelson* reversed course, leaving the convoy to proceed with the remaining Home Fleet cruisers. Desultory bombing continued until dusk, the destroyer *Firedrake* being damaged and having to return.

The Senior Officer of the escort, now Rear-Admiral Syfret aboard *Edinburgh*, ordered two large changes of course under cover of darkness.

1. Tobruk waterfront after an explosion in the ammunition cargo of the small Italian ship lying alongside. Note one of the vessel's cargo winches in the right middle distance. (IWM HU5614)

2. East Africa. A Vickers Wellesley, fitted with underwing bomb containers, is seen over the arid Abyssinian landscape as it returns from a bombing mission against the Italian stronghold at Keren. (IWM CM645)

3. HM Submarine *Olympus* at Malta, storing prior to a patrol. One of an elderly class too large for Mediterranean operations, she was sunk by mine in May 1942. (IWM A6928)

4. Her bow still attached to her mooring and her stern on the bottom of Grand Harbour, HMS *Maori* makes a forlorn sight in February 1942. For several periods the *Luftwaffe* made the base untenable for surface ships. (IWM A9512)

5. The Italian submarine *Uarsciek* settles in the water prior to sinking, December 1942. She had been heavily depth-charged by the British destroyer *Petard* and the Greek *Vasilissa Olga*. (IWM GM2428)

6. With the arrival of the 'Stoneage' convoy in November 1942, Malta's long seige could be said to have ended. Despite the general black-out still evident, the urgent need for cargoes justified the use of the ship's decklights. (IWM GM1927)

7. Noticeably down by the head and with her bows opened out by a torpedo, the cargo liner *Brisbane Star* was one of the survivors of the August convoy. The lifeboats are swung out and the scrambling nets rigged. (IWM GM1436)

8. Following the 'Torch' landings, many valuable British ships were lost while lying offshore. Here, the P&O liner *Cathay* burns to destruction off Bougie. To the left can be seen the monitor HMS *Roberts,* also damaged by bombing. (IWM A12833)

9. A posting at Gibraltar was no sinecure, the Rock being a perfect natural training ground. The pristine condition of these squaddies' shorts, however, suggests a publicity exercise on this occasion. (IWM GM382)

SEVEN

To the Fall of Tobruk

December 1941 to June 1942

'NO AMERICAN will think it wrong of me if I proclaim that to have the United States at our side was to me the greatest joy . . . We had won the war. England would live; Britain would live; the Commonwealth of Nations and the Empire would live.' Prime Minister Churchill's ecstatic words, though written well after the event, capture the relief he must have felt at the time and how he had previously concealed his forebodings.

Although, at this time, the DAK was retreating westwards, the portents in the Mediterranean were not good. Having just suffered its worst-ever run of casualties, the Royal Navy saw the replacements that should have plugged the gaps being sent to the Far East. Almost immediately the battlecruiser *Repulse* and the new battleship *Prince of Wales* were overwhelmed by Japanese torpedo aircraft, deployed, not in the penny-packets available to the FAA, but in numbers that totally defeated any anti-aircraft defence. British military strength in the Far East was woefully inadequate to defend the nation's sprawling imperial interests. The politicians' pre-war bluff well and truly called, this strength had suddenly to be conjured up. Again the forces in the Western Desert were robbed, to the tune of two Australian, one Indian and one British division, while the seasoned 7th Armoured Brigade was sent to Burma.

Churchill might have welcomed the United States' entry into the struggle, but the benefits would be long-term. Potential there was aplenty, but, for the moment, the nation was acting as the Soviet Union had in the previous June, like a wounded giant, crazed with pain, moving and defending with neither plan nor co-ordination. Wasting no time, Churchill sailed for America with a top-level delegation and, at the so-called Arcadia Conference, defined with President Roosevelt the framework for the joint conduct of the war. Joint Chiefs of Staff were also agreed. It came as a welcome surprise to the British that their new ally still regarded Germany as the prime enemy, agreeing that Japan would be contained until Hitler's Reich was defeated.

The implications for the Mediterranean war were far-reaching. First, French North Africa was identified as a useful baseline from which to

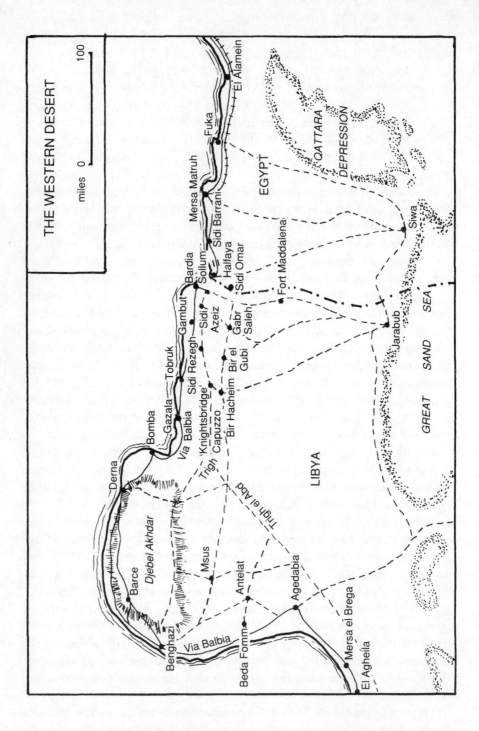

THE WESTERN DESERT

miles

0   100

El Alamein
Fuka
Mersa Matruh
Sidi Barrani
Sollum
Bardia
Halfaya
Sidi Omar
Gambut
Sidi Azeiz
Sidi Rezegh
Gabr Saleh
Fort Maddalena
Tobruk
Gazala
Via Balbia
'Knightsbridge'
Trigh Capuzzo
Bir el Gubi
Bir Hacheim
Bomba
Derna
Djebel Akhdar
Trigh el Abd
Barce
Msus
Antelat
Benghazi
Via Balbia
Beda Fomm
Agedabia
Mersa el Brega
El Agheila
Siwa
Jarabub
GREAT SAND SEA
QATTARA DEPRESSION
EGYPT
LIBYA

commence the reconquest of Europe. Optimistically, Roosevelt and Churchill agreed to land 180,000 troops, half from each power, in the territory 'not later than 25th May 1942'. A British plan, 'Gymnast', already existed, awaiting a politically opportune moment: this was now dusted off and expanded into 'Super Gymnast'. Unfortunately, the power and capability of Japan had been disastrously underestimated and, for the moment, planned timetables counted for little.

In the Western Desert the Axis army continued its retreat, a process which soon gained momentum. It was conducted skilfully, the pursuers, themselves exhausted by extended combat, being kept at a safe distance. Aircraft fuel was becoming a major problem as tankers were sunk, and *Luftwaffe* operations were becoming geared to what fuel could be brought over by Ju 52s or by submarine. On 10 December, for instance, there was aviation fuel sufficient for just one day's flying, and then,on the 12th, came the news of the disaster to the *da Barbiano* and *di Giussano* cruisers carrying emergency supplies.

The DAK resisted at Gazala for five days but, on 15 December, began to move back again. With its armour concentrated and continuously protected by an anti-tank screen, it avoided significant confrontation. Rommel reported thus: 'After four weeks of uninterrupted and costly fighting, the fighting power of the troops . . . is showing signs of flagging, all the more so as the supply of arms and ammunition has completely dried up . . .' Concerned at the political consequences of abandoning Cyrenaica, the Italians had a high-level joint delegation visit Rommel. The latter remained unmoved, pointing out bluntly that there was no question of making a stand and that only by preserving his forces in good order could he hope eventually to defend Tripolitania from stronger ground.

By 22 December the DAK was back to Beda Fomm and Antelat; a further 45 new tanks had arrived at Tripoli but an equal number had been sunk en route. After inflicting a sharp reverse on the British near Antelat, where the latter lost 60 tanks out of 110 deployed, the DAK reached its chosen defensive positions near Agheila. It was in good heart, having conducted a long and difficult retreat without destroying or abandoning its equipment. Its logistics lines were now short and secure, while those of the British were attenuated. As a result of recent setbacks by the Royal Navy (particularly to Force 'K'), supply ships were also getting through in larger numbers, a process assisted by Kesselring's *Luftflotte II* in its raids on Malta.

Rommel's amazing energy now showed itself. His wireless intercept service was very efficient and quickly noted the absence of the more experienced British units, withdrawn for dispatch to the Far East. Until the British had time to move up and consolidate, there thus appeared to be a short period in which the Axis actually had local superiority. Informing neither his Italian superior nor his own High Command, Rommel made unobtrusive re-dispositions, largely by night. 'I daren't say anything . . . They'd think me crazy. But I'm not, I simply see a bit further than they do . . . ,' he confided in a private letter.

He would have been even more heartened had he known of the British strategic view. On 19 December Auchinleck concurred with Ritchie's opinion that the offensive could not be renewed before mid-February, but, in the long term, the C-in-C had it as his view that, if Rommel could not be penned west of his present line, he would consider withdrawing all the way back to the Egyptian border: 'It is not my intention to hold permanently Tobruk or any other locality west of the frontier.' For a second time the British had been within an ace of ejecting the Axis from North Africa, but for a second time they had been frustrated by the higher-priority needs of another theatre.

Rommel's security measures paid off handsomely, particularly as the Axis High Command, not knowing of his plans, generated no radio traffic which the British could intercept. The latter were also unaware that 55 new tanks had just arrived for the DAK in a convoy that docked in Tripoli on 5 January. Six transports had been run by the Italians with a massive fleet cover of four battleships, six cruisers, 24 destroyers and eleven pre-positioned submarines. This operation had consumed a large proportion of the Fleet's oil reserves, but in a cause that allowed Rommel to resume the offensive. Ironically, although British submarines and aircraft reported sightings, there existed no means to take any firm action. The few available surface forces were engaged at the time with the necessary passage and return of the *Glengyle* and *Breconshire* to and from Malta.

During this period the Italians conducted 46 submarine missions to North Africa with cased fuel. The inflammability of the cargo was complemented by the generation of toxic and explosive vapour which could be ventilated only by risky surface-running. It was due to such circumstances that *Upholder* sank the new *Ammiraglio Saint-Bon* off Sicily during the night of 5/6 January and the 'Hunt' class *Farndale* her sister, *Ammiraglio Caracciolo*, off Bardia. Results, nevertheless, encouraged the Italians to embark on the construction of a series of cargo-only submarines (as the Germans and Japanese had done).

A revitalized Rommel struck back on 21 January against a much reduced and disparate collection of British formations. Again it was the latter's turn to yield ground but, though the DAK made a rapid advance, its efforts to surround and eliminate British armour were unsuccessful. This was because the situation changed so rapidly that the army was literally ahead of its intelligence.

General Cavellero, backed by Kesselring, tried to get Rommel to drop the risky thrust into Cyrenaica. Both were brusquely answered and, less the Italians (pulled out by Cavellero), the DAK roared on. Little worried by a Royal Air Force again grounded by the weather, it took Msus on the 25th. The inexperienced British formation lost, in just the forenoon, nearly 100 tanks, 38 guns and 190 lorries, but what could have turned into a rout was again limited by the DAK's outrunning its fuel supplies. Frustrated in his attempt to drive straight across the chord of Cyrenaica, Rommel diverted forces to feint towards Mechili while he, in heavy rain, thrust at Benghazi from the east. On 29 January this important port was again in Axis hands. Tripoli, its vital partner, was again beyond British bombing range, except from a denuded Malta.

Early in February, with his logistics bordering on the chaotic, Rommel came to a halt, enabling the Eighth Army to stabilize along the line Gazala–Bir Hacheim. He was well satisfied, having regained at little cost most of the ground that he had recently voluntarily relinquished. He was rewarded by promotion to Colonel-General, while in the British camp recriminations abounded. London was dismayed at how simply the gains of 'Crusader' had been lost and how the quality of the armour and the tactical proficiency of its commanders seemed inferior to those of the enemy. Differences arose between the Army Commander and his Corps commanders, while the Army itself was totally disillusioned at the manner in which it was being led. All this was known to Rommel who, estimating the British to be beyond making any further offensive move for about two months, planned his next move.

Meanwhile Malta's reduced circumstances were reflected in Italian convoy delivery figures: in December 39,000 tons were landed, in January 66,000 tons and in February/March 107,000 tons. Less than 20,000 tons were lost en route, mostly to submarine attack. During January 1942, as already noted, the island received useful deliveries from the *Breconshire* and *Glengyle*, each of which offloaded 10,000 tons. A four-ship convoy was also run from Alexandria under the direction of Rear-Admiral Vian. Departing on the 16th, it arrived less the Norwegian freighter *Thermopylae* (which had included ten tanks and sixteen anti-aircraft guns in her manifest) and the destroyer *Gurkha*, torpedoed by *U133*.

'Ultra' indicated the imminent passage of large Italian convoy, but Malta, having suffered a total of 262 air raids during January alone, could do little to dispute it. In fact, heartened by Rommel's success, the Italians were running four freighters and the passenger liner *Victoria* (an odd mix with a significant difference in speed) under heavy cover. Aboard the liner were 1,600 German troops, while 73 tanks were included in the cargoes of the remainder. High-level bombing was staged from Cyrenaican and Egyptian airfields, but it was the début of torpedo-carrying Beauforts that proved effective, one cargo ship being sunk and the 13,000-ton *Victoria* halted. FAA Albacores, operating from Benghazi, finished the latter off. Within days, however, these airfields had all fallen to the DAK and such strikes were no longer possible.

Diminished capacity was soon apparent. On 12 February, with the Eighth Army back on the Gazala line, a further three ships were sailed from Alexandria for Malta. Deliberately in two groups, they steered as though making coastwise for Tobruk. Beyond this point they could no longer enjoy air cover, so the escort included the anti-aircraft cruiser *Carlisle* and seven 'Hunts', all with high-angle armament. Despite a 'colossal' expenditure of 4in ammunition, all three ships were lost by bombing attack.

During February 1942 the Axis flew 3,100 sorties against Malta. Only one or two dozen Hurricanes were serviceable at any time. All were Mk IIs, whose 0.303 machine guns were no longer adequate to deal with the Ju 88s, which were now fitted with extra protection. The defenders were now also outperformed by the *Luftwaffe*'s Me 109Fs and the Italian Reggianes with German-designed engines. The AOC Malta, Air Vice-Marshal Lloyd, made an appeal for cannon-armed fighters to deal with the Ju 88s and for Spitfires to counter their escort.

Help came for an unexpected reason. A powerful German surface squadron built around the fast battleships *Scharnhorst* and *Gneisenau* and the heavy cruiser *Prinz Eugen* had, for some time, been based on the French Atlantic port of Brest. Posing a considerable threat, the group greatly influenced the mobility of not only the Home Fleet but also Force 'H' at Gibraltar. In February 1942 the Germans boldly broke out to their bases via the English Channel. While their escape was lamentable, their absence greatly lightened the responsibilities of Force 'H': now under the command of Rear-Admiral Syfret, it could devote more time to Mediterranean matters.

Since the loss of *Ark Royal*, no fighter ferrying trips had been made to Malta, but no fewer than three runs were made during March. These were with the Spitfires desperately needed by Lloyd, but, though *Eagle* made three trips and *Argus* one, only 31 fighters could be accommodated in total because of their fixed-wing configuration. A shortage of spare parts, particularly engines, and a dearth of skilled ground crews also militated against instant miracles, but it was a start.

The scale of the *Luftwaffe*'s effort against Malta suggested the approach of some sort of climax, and, indeed, Kesselring had finally obtained the *Führer*'s approval for the island's capture. This, Operation 'Herkules', would be a joint Axis affair, timed for June or July 1942. Malta's three primary airfields were to be continually suppressed by the use of heavy and anti-personnel bombs, strafing and nuisance raids by night to hinder repairs and to wear down personnel. Every effort was to be made to sink every supply ship by dive-bombing or mining. Great privation began as all food stocks diminished. Captain Simpson's submarines were obliged to spend daylight hours sweltering on the harbour bottom. Repairs were made largely by night but were still interrupted by raids and slowed by the undernourishment of the dockyard men.

As Malta's pulse slowed, Churchill bombarded Auchinleck with demands for an early offensive to retake Cyrenaica and enable a westbound convoy to be run to the island. Determined that 'Crusader''s mistakes would not be repeated, Auchinleck obstinately demanded a superiority in armour of three to two, and time to strengthen Tobruk and the Gazala line. If forward dumps could be created, he would move on 1 May.

With the situation in the Far East deteriorating, the Premier was not pleased. He sent the Vice-CIGS and the Lord Privy Seal to pressurize the C-in-C, hinting also that, as he was not using them profitably, fifteen air squadrons would be transferred. Auchinleck, unmoved, succeeded in swinging his influential visitors to his point of view. Turning the strategic question on its head, he queried the relevance of Malta to his situation in North Africa. A signal from London icily set him straight: Malta had the priority. Implicit was the certainty of dismissal if London's authority were again to be challenged.

Malta's situation was by now so grave that a convoy had to be risked, with or without military success in Cyrenaica. In advance of the movement, cruisers bombed enemy airfields in the Dodecanese in an effort to have *Luftwaffe* strength transferred there. The Royal Air Force attacked airfields used by reconnaissance flights, while on 20 March, the day that the convoy sailed, the Army made feints in the direction of forward Axis airfields. Four merchant ships were covered by a close escort comprising *Carlisle*, seven 'Hunts' and six destroyers. Rear-Admiral Vian, with three *Dido* class cruisers and four destroyers, provided distant cover, in company with *Penelope* and a destroyer—all that remained of Force 'K'. A total of 23 escorts sounds impressive until it is remembered that *Penelope*'s six 6in guns were the heaviest available. Admiral Cunningham had been informed by the Chiefs of Staff that 'no consideration of risk to ships need deter you'. The 'Hunts' were sent in advance along the African coast on an anti-submarine sweep, only themselves to be ambushed, losing *Heythrop* to a torpedo from *U562*.

Vian's progress was uneventful until he was sighted by a pair of patrolling Italian submarines when north of Derna in the afternoon of the 21st. *Supermarina* responded by sailing the battleship *Littorio* and four destroyers from Taranto. These were to rendezvous with three cruisers and four more destroyers from Messina. The Taranto group was reported as it sailed by the submarine *P36*, giving warning to Vian that, where air attack could be expected from daybreak on the 22nd, surface attack was likely in the afternoon. Well aware of its importance to Malta, Vian was determined to fight the convoy through. To this end, he organized its escort in five mutually supportive groups. Five 'Hunts' would remain close to the merchantmen to give anti-aircraft cover while *Carlisle* and another 'Hunt' would lay a continuous smokescreen. The remainder would repel the surface attack.

By 0800 on the 22nd the convoy had passed the meridian of Benghazi, the current limit of fighter cover. Within the next 90 minutes Italian and German aircraft flew an estimated 150 sorties against it, without success. Admiral Iachino, aboard *Littorio*, was meanwhile pushing southwards, his speed limited to 22kts by a rising south-easterly gale. His destroyers were labouring, and one, *Grecale*, turned back with machinery problems. The three Italian cruisers were posted ahead on a line of search but were already on the convoy's quarter when an aircraft spotted it and dropped flares. These were observed by the British also. The time was 1330 and the opposing sides were about 35 miles apart.

Soon after 1400 the wing ship, *Euryalus*, reported smoke to the north, followed by a visual sighting report at 1427. What were apparently three Italian battleships revealed themselves, to British relief, as cruisers when they turned back on the as yet unsighted *Littorio*, in an effort at enticement. As pre-arranged, the convoy turned away on to a south-westerly heading, the instantly laid smokescreen being seized by the wind, rolling down towards the advancing Italians as a thin but opaque curtain.

Two Italian cruisers opened 8in fire from an ineffective range of over twelve miles. The British cruiser captains, already well out-ranged, kept approximate station on the convoy. During this opening phase, which concluded at 1535, high- and low-level bombing attacks were also delivered. No damage was done, but the escort's high-angle ammunition was greatly depleted.

In fast-deteriorating weather, the Italians concentrated at 1618. Wind speeds were now 30kts and increasing. Ships were moving uncomfortably, taking aboard solid water and washed overall by curtains of wind-driven spray. Vian endeavoured to bring the convoy back on to the direct route to Malta, shielded by further ships making smoke. At 1700 it became apparent that the enemy was trying to work around the head of the British to see beyond the smoke barrier. For two and a half hours he was thwarted by escorts laying smoke on opportunity and darting in and out of the pall to threaten torpedo attack while monitoring Iachino's dispositions. It was a high-risk strategy, however, and several British ships were caught at uncomfortably close ranges. Fifteen personnel were killed when a 6in shell struck the bridge of the flagship, *Cleopatra*, while her sister, *Euryalus*, suffered extensive superficial damage from a straddle by a 15in salvo. Hit and badly damaged by what was probably an 8in projectile, the destroyer *Kingston* could only launch her remaining torpedoes and drop out.

At 1800, the poor conditions no longer allowing him to account for all known Italian units, Vian dashed over to the convoy to assure himself that all was well. During his absence, his destroyers worked the harder, *Havock* surviving a hit by a 15in shell. Iachino had pushed to within eight miles of the convoy, and every available escort was involved in 'fierce-face' tactics, darting in and out of the fog of smoke. Most had long since released all their torpedoes, but the threat was sufficient. All had missed in the conditions, and wildly gyrating decks had made gunnery equally ineffective, only one British shell scoring a hit.

What was important was that the veiled sun was now dipping towards the western horizon. Every destroyer that still possessed a torpedo was pressed into one last desperate effort at 1845. Emerging from the murk, they launched a spread of twenty-five, clearly visible to the enemy, only 6,000yds away. The silhouettes of Iachino's ships shortened as one, as they turned away together on a northerly heading. Mercifully, they did not turn back, and by 1858 firing had ceased.

Bold tactics and the expenditure of a prodigious quantity of ammunition had served Vian well. Unscathed, the convoy was still heading for Malta, though greatly delayed. Bearing in mind the weather, this meant that it would not be safe at Valletta by daybreak. Satisfied that the Italians would not return to renew the fight after dark, Vian turned back at 1940 for Alexandria. Four of his destroyers, damaged, went on with the convoy escort, it being less risky in the conditions.

The following morning, that of the 23rd, the *Luftwaffe* mounted a major effort, but by 1000 the Norwegian *Talabot* and the British *Pampas* were in Grand Harbour, the latter with two unexploded bombs aboard. Still eight miles offshore, the veteran *Breconshire* was hit and immobilized: on her eighth run to the island, her luck had run out. Heavy seas frustrated an attempt by *Penelope* to take her in tow, so she was anchored, covered by three 'Hunts'. The fourth ship, *Clan Campbell*, was not yet in sight of Malta when, at about 1030, she was bombed from mast height. She foundered quickly, her survivors being rescued with difficulty by *Eridge*, but the destroyer *Legion*, sent to assist, was so badly shaken by a near-miss that she had to be beached. She was later brought around to Valletta, only to be sunk there by bombing. Watching over the stricken *Breconshire*, the *Southwold* ran over a mine and was destroyed. With an improvement in the weather, the big cargo vessel was brought around to her usual anchorage of Marsaxlokk, only to be bombed again. Well ablaze, she rolled over on the 27th, leaving one bilge exposed. As a final service to the island, she provided a source of fuel oil, which was pumped out through valves let into her hull.

Both the *Talabot* and the *Pampas* were heavily bombed at their berths. With much ammunition aboard, the Norwegian was scuttled as a precaution. The *Pampas* had three of her five holds flooded and much of her precious cargo ruined. Of the 26,000 tons delivered, only 5,000 were safely unloaded, and there was much justified criticism of rates and methods of unloading. As a matter of urgency, procedures were tightened.

In what became known as the Second Battle of Sirte, the British losses were considerable and the stresses of the weather caused more problems for Vian's ships as they returned to Alexandria. The damaged *Lively* had to be diverted to Tobruk. The Italians, in withdrawing, passed through the peak of the storm's severity to the east of Sicily. Two destroyers, *Scirocco* and *Lanciere*, were overwhelmed and sunk by the conditions.

Admiral Cunningham rightly considered Second Sirte as 'one of the most brilliant actions of the war, if not the most brilliant', but had to advise the Admiralty that, as of 26 March, he possessed just two serviceable fleet destroyers. The generally larger Italians, with the seas on their port bows, had made far steadier gun platforms than the small British vessels, which were corkscrewing and yawing in a quartering sea. What decided the day, however, was not gunnery but resolution, and Vian richly merited the knighthood that was bestowed upon him.

A personal blow to the Mediterranean Fleet at this time was the appointment of Admiral Cunningham as representative of the First Sea Lord on the Combined Chiefs of Staff Committee in Washington. Though at times irascible and even downright unreasonable, he had led the Fleet well through severe trials. He departed on 3 April 1942, leaving Vice-Admiral Pridham-Wippell to act as caretaker until the arrival of the new C-in-C, Admiral Sir Henry Harwood (of River Plate fame).

The Fleet itself was not in good shape. At Alexandria there were just four cruisers and fifteen destroyers operational. Crews were tired, and the enemy seemed to enjoy superiority everywhere except in morale. At the Gibraltar end, Force 'H' was absent for operations in Madagascar, leaving only the venerable carrier *Argus*, incapable of offensive use, and a handful of destroyers. The Royal Navy faced an Italian Fleet estimated on 1 April 1942 to include four battleships, nine cruisers and 55 destroyers and torpedo boats. In addition, there were fifty Italian and twenty German submarines in the theatre, while about 540 Axis bombers were grouped for operations in the Central and Eastern Mediterranean.

Following the loss of so much cargo in the March convoy, a further attempt needed to be made quickly. A first step was to bolster the number of Spitfires on the island. The carrier *Eagle* was in dock, however, while

Victorious's lifts could not accommodate the fixed-wing fighters. *Argus* was too small and slow for the task. Unusually, an American carrier, *Wasp*, was in Scottish waters, and a request direct from the Prime Minister to the President was successful in gaining her services (though with the rider that the Americans noted that the plans of HMS *Furious* showed lifts large enough to take a Spitfire). Leaving Greenock on 14 April, *Wasp* flew off 47 fighters on the 20th (Operation 'Calendar'). All but one arrived safely but, such was the scale of fighting over the island, these were reduced to just six within a matter of four days. During April, nearly 7,000 tons of bombs had been rained on Malta by Kesselring's aircraft.

Churchill was obliged to seek Roosevelt's help a second time, and on 9 May *Wasp* and *Eagle* together flew off a total of 64 Spitfires (Operation 'Bowery'). Sixty arrived safely. At a time when the Americans were hard put to contain the Japanese juggernaut in the Pacific, it had been a generous gesture, and the Royal Navy was pleased to be able to repay the debt when, following the Battle of Santa Cruz in October 1942, the US Navy itself was short of flight decks. This response was made at considerable cost as the British Home Fleet was left with no carrier at all—a situation remedied by relieving the Mediterranean Fleet of *Formidable*.

A source of intelligence upon which the Axis placed much credence was the decyphering of routine reports sent to the United States by their Military Attaché in Cairo. In April he described how run down was the RAF's strength on Malta, how the island had been abandoned by the surface fleet and how it was dependent now upon submarine-delivered necessities. He estimated that, at the beginning of April, Malta had just seven weeks' supplies remaining and, since the British were 'too weak to seize Benghazi prior to June 1st . . . it is therefore too late to save Malta'. Extra significance was added by the classification of the report, which was not for British eyes. Paradoxically, this worked in favour of the British. Meeting in Austria, the two dictators complacently assumed that, as Malta was ripe for plucking, it could wait while support was given to a Rommel offensive in late May. With Tobruk taken, the DAK would halt at the Egyptian frontier, allowing their massive air support to be returned to Sicily for yet another 'final' reduction of the island prior to its invasion.

Incredibly, Malta was thus granted a further reprieve as the *Luftwaffe* was sent to North Africa in support of Rommel. The island was by now so devastated that the Germans 'hardly knew where to drop their bombs'. Once a secure haven, Grand Harbour was becoming littered with wrecks. The bows of the destroyer *Maori* protruded from the oil-streaked water, still attached to their mooring buoy. Nearby lay the abandoned after end of *Gallant*, which had lost her bows to a mine a year previously. *Legion* was towed in damaged but finally sunk in an air raid on 26 March. Ten days later her sister, *Lance*, was damaged beyond economic repair while in dry dock. The next to succumb was *Kingston* which, being repaired following splinter damage at Second Sirte, was hit by bombs three times in six days.

Some escaped. Force 'K''s light cruiser *Penelope* was trapped in dry dock by a bomb-damaged caisson. For days the ship acted as a stationary anti-aircraft battery as all available hands fought to stop the dock flooding and the ship incurring fatal cumulative bomb damage. Finally, her thin hide bristling with wooden plugs applied to a thousand splinter holes, she sailed for Gibraltar. The destroyer *Havock* was also patched up sufficiently to allow her to make a run for Gibraltar. In order to avoid minefields she hugged the Tunisian coast, but, steaming at 30kts and with over a hundred passengers aboard, she hit a sandbank and was wrecked. The hulk was blown up and all personnel passed into Vichy French internment.

The Malta-based submarines chalked up a success when *Urge* caught the light cruiser *Giovanni delle Bande Nere* north of the Messina Strait. Damaged by weather at Second Sirte, the ship was bound for repair at La Spezia when blown in two on 1 April. Within the space of a few days, however, three submarines—*P36*, *Pandora* and the Greek *Glavkos*—were sunk by bombing at Valletta. *Pandora* was discharging a cargo of spare torpedoes. In addition *Unbeaten*, lying submerged alongside, was damaged by a near-miss to the extent that her distorted tubes could no longer be used. Captain Simpson, already highly critical at the slow build-up of fighters to protect the island, and dismayed at the ease with which their operational strength could be diminished, was convinced that his scale of losses could no longer be tolerated. An operational patrol was becoming less risky than a spell of rest and refit in the submarine base—literally.

Further hard blows were imminent. Having sunk two destroyers, two submarines and nearly 100,000 tons of shipping in a tragically short career, Lt-Cdr Wanklyn, VC, DSO, and his *Upholder* went missing in April. In the first week of May *Urge* was sunk. Though mines were suspected, it transpired eventually that both boats had fallen victim to the Italian torpedo boat *Pegaso*. Finally, *Olympus* was sunk on a mine just beyond the Valletta entrance. German E-boats, working from the small Sicilian port of Licata, were mining the approaches almost nightly. Lacking were the cannon-equipped Beaufighters to deter them and the minesweepers with which to counter them. It was time to go. Simpson explained to the Senior Naval Officer that, if his remaining boats did not pull out, they would stay for good. During the closing days of April the 10th Flotilla therefore redeployed temporarily to Alexandria.

It was at this time that 40 *Luftwaffe* dive-bombers and 45 fighters were transferred to North Africa and 60 Spitfires arrived at Malta by courtesy of *Wasp* and *Eagle*. These were turned around rapidly to avoid their being caught on the ground, as had many of *Wasp*'s first delivery. The Germans took the view that, as Malta was no longer interfering with North African convoys, they had achieved their aim and it was time to move on. As a decision it was militarily inept.

On 10 May the fast minelayer *Welshman* ran in a substantial cargo of ammunition. It seemed to mark a watershed, and, with the air raids obviously being scaled down, the defenders began to feel that their time had perhaps not yet come after all. They were not, of course, to know that Operation '*Herkules*' was due to be mounted as soon as Rommel had taken Tobruk.

For the Royal Navy there was no let up. Both sides in the Western Desert were preparing an offensive, and the DAK's supply system had to be suppressed. With Malta almost impotent, an Axis convoy was detected passing only 85 miles away. The Royal Air Force flew Blenheims and Beauforts against it from its most forward airfields, now east of Gazala. As single-engine fighters lacked the necessary range, the bombers went unescorted, losing six of their number to the Me 110s covering the convoy.

This setback resulted in a destroyer raid being mounted from Alexandria. 'Ultra' indicated that three large merchantmen and three destroyers would arrive at Benghazi on 12 May. Four large destroyers under Captain Poland were routed along the median line of the 200-mile gap between Crete and Cyrenaica. No fighter cover was given, in order to avoid long-range radar detection of the group. Poland's instructions from the new C-in-C were that if he were to be observed, or if he were to be late at the planned intercept, he should return.

Thus when Poland's own ship, *Jervis*, picked up the presence of a reconnaissance aircraft on the afternoon of the 11th, course was reversed and fighter cover requested. Two Beaufighters arrived at about 1630, almost simultaneously with eight Ju 88s. These latter were veterans, coming in low and fast following steep dives from about 12,000ft. Within minutes the enemy was gone, leaving *Lively* foundering from the concussive effect of two very near misses.

A second attack was broken up by the aerial escort, but a third, at 2000, came in out of a brilliant sunset. *Kipling*, hit hard, sank within ten minutes, while *Jackal*, blazing uncontrollably and with a ruptured fuel tank, was taken in tow by *Jervis*. Poland already had 600 survivors aboard his ship and, not willing to risk them further, took off *Jackal*'s crew and sank the crippled vessel by torpedo. Three large destroyers had been expended for no return.

A couple of nights later the Italian submarine *Ambra* launched three 'human torpedoes' outside Alexandria. As the battleship *Queen Elizabeth* still occupied the floating dock and the large submarine depot ship *Medway* was present, countermeasures had been stepped up. Searchlights and explosive charges disorientated the swimmers, all of whom scuttled their vehicles and were made prisoner (although one succeeded in remaining at large in Alexandria for over a month before being apprehended).

On the day before *Wasp*'s second delivery there was a change of governorship in Malta. General Sir William Dobbie had endured openly the same hardships as the population. He was highly regarded but was now in deteriorating health, largely as a result of his responsibilities. The War Cabinet therefore relieved him, and his replacement was Lord Gort, who moved over from Gibraltar. Gort, described by Churchill as 'a warrior of the truest mettle', was a holder of the Victoria Cross and the DSO, with nine Mentions in Dispatches. He was best known for his contribution to the saving of the British Expeditionary Force at Dunkirk. The sudden influx of Spitfires hit Kesselring hard. Between 10 and 12 May the Axis air forces lost more bombers than over the five weeks of the recent all-out offensive, during which a total of 11,500 sorties had been flown.

Churchill believed that the siege could best be lifted by regaining control of Cyrenaica as soon as possible but was obliged to exchange a series of increasingly acrimonious signals with Auchinleck, who refused to be rushed. General Ritchie, convinced that he would be beaten to the draw by Rommel, built up the 40-mile Gazala Line defences, behind which preparations would be made for the Eighth Army's assault. The C-in-C, to match what he saw as superior German flexibility, reorganized fighting formations around three-battalion brigade groups; these could be 'armoured', 'motorized' or 'infantry'. One group garrisoned each of the mutually supportive 'boxes' that comprised the Gazala Line. Shortages resulted in over-large gaps between some boxes. These were filled with minefields, the mines for which were largely lifted from the Tobruk boundary. There was, moreover, insufficient artillery to cover much of the mined area.

The defenders of the Gazala Line were supported by two Armoured Divisions, the 1st and the 7th, which, between them, deployed about 850 serviceable tanks. About 250 of these were newly arrived Grants, whose turret-mounted 37mm armour-piercing gun was supplemented by a 75mm weapon in a starboard-side sponson. The arrangement made for a high-profile tank but one with real hitting power. Of some 560 Axis tanks, about 60 per cent were German, belonging to the 15th and 21st Panzer Divisions. About a score of these vehicles were upgraded Pz IIIs, with a longer-barrelled 50mm gun that had a muzzle velocity capable of defeating a Grant. To offset the supremacy of the 88mm mobile guns to some extent, the British were now receiving the long-awaited 6pdr anti-tank gun. Reckoned either by quantity or quality, however, the Axis air forces held most of the cards.

Auchinleck and Ritchie differed in their reading of Rommel's intentions. The C-in-C thought that a diversionary attack was likely, followed by a swift armoured thrust to divide the Gazala Line in two, one section of which would then be 'rolled up'. Ritchie believed that the German commander would conform to his usual practice, loosing his mobile forces in a sudden outflanking move around the southern end of the line, held by General Koenig's 1st Free French Brigade in the Bir Hacheim box.

On 24 April 'Ultra' came up with a signal from Kesselring which mentioned that the British attack was not likely before 1 June, which would be 'too late'. This indication of an earlier Axis offensive was confirmed by a further intercept which instructed Kesselring's headquarters in Sicily to expect a 'most secret' communication during the evening of 25 May. What became known as the Battle of Gazala was, therefore, not entirely unexpected by the British when it opened on 26 May.

There were also no tactical surprises. A major diversionary attack was staged at the right, or seaward, end of the British line. Then, towards dusk, large numbers of Axis vehicles were headed apparently for Bir Hacheim. They did not leaguer at nightfall, however, and by dawn on the 27th had rounded the British left flank and run into an Indian Motorized Brigade Group and a British Armoured Brigade Group to its left. Both formations fought well, though not fully deployed, but, even though they inflicted loss on the enemy, both were obliged to fall back.

Like the 7th Armoured Division, the 1st had also indulged in the British habit of separating its two Brigade Groups. These, as part of the mobile reserve, were ordered to meet Rommel's flying column. They were still not concentrated when they ran into two panzer divisions and, despite the hitting power of their Grants, were brushed aside with the loss of thirty tanks.

Flushed with success, the DAK raced on, intent on reaching Acroma, at which point it would wheel left and hit the Gazala Line from the rear. Its speed, however, once again resulted in a loss of cohesion and, during the afternoon, in the neighbourhood of the 'Knightsbridge' box, it was hit in either flank by unco-ordinated but effective British armoured attacks.

The DAK broke in confusion and, as darkness fell over the battlefields on the 27th, Rommel's situation was far from healthy. His habit of over-extending himself had rebounded on him. He had already lost one-third of his tanks, while the remainder were low on fuel and ammunition. On a personal level, his situation left him out of touch with much of both the battle and his staff. The Italian Ariete Armoured Division, tasked with reducing Koenig's brigade at Bir Hacheim, had so far failed. Between the French and the British, farther east at Bir el Gubi, all of Rommel's supply columns had to pass. If the Eighth Army could close this gap it would effectively isolate a large proportion of the DAK, though keeping so powerful a force from breaking out again would be a different matter. Rommel saved the day on the 28th by attacking with the 21st Panzers, the only armoured division which had sufficient remaining fuel. This unexpected move unbalanced the British, who spent the day involved, for the most part, in small-scale and desultory skirmishing or actually remaining disengaged.

In this most confused of situations the British, had they concentrated their armour, could have scored a major victory. For their part, the Italians had cleared a breach through the unsupported minefields to the north of Bir Hacheim, but neither the British nor the DAK appeared aware of it. Rommel was totally out of touch with his senior commanders and could not be contacted. Lt-Gen Cruewell, anxious to find his commander, flew down in a light aircraft, only to be brought down and captured. Thus it was that Field Marshal Kesselring, who was visiting at the time, was requested to stand in as temporary DAK commander. It was an object lesson to him, learning as he did 'the difficulties of a commander whose hands are tied by subordination to the headquarters that issues no orders and cannot be reached . . .'

Most of the 29th was characterized by a series of unco-ordinated clashes around the 'Knightsbridge' box. With his armour concentrated and again fully supplied, Rommel resolved to escape from the pocket into which he had forced himself by punching westwards through the Gazala Line, i.e. from its rear. His chosen course was to reduce both the Free French box and that of the British 150th Brigade Group adjacent to the north.

As the British higher command was preoccupied with its own plans for attack, the plight of the 150th went unnoticed. Unsupported, it fought literally to the last round on 31 May and 1 June before it was simply overwhelmed. Rommel had opened his gap and also isolated Koenig at Bir Hacheim. The latter held on for ten days in a well-prepared position, conducting a battle of what the German commander himself described as 'extraordinary severity'.

General Auchinleck was still expecting a British break-out westwards from the Gazala Line, but Ritchie, reasonably, wanted the substantial Axis armour behind him to be neutralized first. As the Eighth Army still had a fair superiority in tanks, this appeared to be no great problem. The plan apparently co-ordinated correctly the armour, artillery and anti-tank units but, in doing so, created a unwieldly command structure. Rommel anticipated such an attack and made his move on 11 June, the day after the survivors of the Bir Hacheim had been evacuated. His first instinct was to form a 'hedgehog', an armoured defensive ring against which the British could expend their strength, but, forewarned by radio intercepts, the latter did not oblige. Neither, unfortunately, did they do much else, as Ritchie's Corps commanders were engaged in a difference of opinion.

Inevitably, the DAK changed over to attack and, in hazy weather, hit the British armour with both panzer divisions, penning them into the 'Knightsbridge' box with the loss of about 120 tanks. On the 13th the box itself was abandoned. With the situation deteriorating rapidly, Ritchie proposed cutting his losses by pulling his forces back 30 miles from the Gazala positions to the Tobruk perimeter. Auchinleck agreed, stating that Tobruk must be held but must not be allowed to become invested again.

However, while Ritchie was agreeing one plan with his C-in-C, his more experienced subordinates, especially Gott, were intent on withdrawing all the way to the Egyptian frontier. They had informed Ritchie of this intention and, with British armour reduced to about 70 tanks, there appeared little option to either yielding Tobruk or accepting another siege. The Prime Minister then signalled Auchinleck on the importance of holding the fortress. Both the C-in-C and Ritchie began to send increasingly vaguely worded communications, it becoming obvious that the forces that would be required to hold Tobruk were already headed back for the frontier in what was later referred to as the 'Gazala Gallop'. Ritchie finally bluntly informed his C-in-C's representative that, in the circumstances, he could not confidently stand and fight.

In view of the disorganized state of the Eighth Army, the withdrawal was proceeding remarkably well, owing, in no small measure, to the equal exhaustion of the enemy. Tobruk was still in British hands, though any uncertainty regarding whether or how it was to be held was quickly resolved by Rommel. Long intent on the removal of what he referred to as 'the symbol of British resistance' he whipped his forces into a quick attack. Between 16 amd 18 June he took key points beyond the perimeter and successfully accounted for the greater part of the remaining scratch units of British armour.

During the night of the 17th/18th, German tanks reached the coast, west of Gazala, technically cutting off Tobruk once again. The Royal Air Force was obliged hurriedly to abandon the valuable forward airstrips around Gambut, and both at these and at partially cleared or destroyed dumps, the enemy recovered large quantities of fuel, rations and transport—even 'fifteen serviceable aircraft'. With Tobruk 'temporarily' invested, though by a force whose strength grew with each passing hour,

Auchinleck and Ritchie conferred; however, decisions were made at Army and Corps level, confirming Rommel's long-held opinion that the British command structure was 'never very quick at reorganizing' and could always be wrong-footed by a fluid and adaptive attack.

Tobruk's capacity to resist had been considerably reduced. Combat troops amounted to about five brigades. Two of these were South African, whose Maj-Gen Klopper was also the garrison commander. There were roughly 60 tanks and considerable artillery assets, but vast numbers of mines had been recovered from the defences, purloined for use mainly at Gazala. It was thought by both Auchinleck and Ritchie that Tobruk would be assaulted from the east, the latter signalling cheerfully to Klopper that, whether the DAK attacked Tobruk or the border, the garrison of the other would be able to strike at the enemy rear. The C-in-C, convinced that Rommel would act quickly, was 'perturbed' at the deliberate nature of the preparations being made to meet the threat: 'Crisis may arise in a matter of hours, not days . . .'

He was right on all counts. A feint was staged by an Italian corps at the south-western corner of the perimeter during the night of 19/20 June. At first light the *Luftwaffe* pounded the south-eastern corner. A creeping bombardment then swept over the defenders in this sector; they emerged, dazed, to find the German infantry already overrunning them. Within three hours the two panzer divisions were sweeping through the gap. Rommel and his Chiefs of Staff were right up with them.

Despite the power of the attack, Klopper was not convinced that it was the enemy's main thrust and was reluctant to commit his reserves. It was late morning before the British armour came into action, immediately finding itself outnumbered three to one. It was virtually wiped out, whereupon the enemy tanks closed the supporting artillery to point-blank range, eliminating it largely by machine-gun fire levelled at the now unprotected gun crews.

By early afternoon the DAK held the high ground that commanded the town and the brief battle entered its final phase. In their advance, several German tanks were knocked out by British 3.7in heavy anti-aircraft guns being used in the low-angle role pioneered so successfully by the enemy 88mm. At 1800, as the enemy armour entered the town, the defenders began to destroy their equipment. Much of use was destroyed prematurely, hastening the confusion and the inevitable climax. With the dawn of 21 June the white flag was raised and Klopper, his staff and 32,000 men passed into captivity. Many outposts refused to believe the surrender, commandeered transport and escaped by simply driving eastwards across the desert.

Though run down, Tobruk was still powerfully symbolic, and Rommel claimed its capture as the crowning achievement of his career. At a point when deliveries of supplies to the DAK were well below requirements, the booty included an estimated 2,000 tons of fuel, 2,000 serviceable vehicles and 5,000 tons of provisions. Rommel was elevated by his *Führer* to the rank of Field Marshal.

EIGHT

To First Alamein

June 1942 to August 1942

PRIME MINISTER Churchill had flown to Washington and was quartered in the White House for discussions with President Roosevelt. Their meeting was interrupted by the arrival of a telegram. The President scanned it and handed it to the Premier without comment. It read, simply, 'Tobruk has surrendered, with 25,000 [*sic*] men taken prisoner'. Unbelieving, Churchill had General Ismay check with London. Within minutes, however, came separate confirmation from Admiral Harwood, the new C-in-C, Mediterranean. As dive-bombers would now be able to concentrate on Alexandria, flying with fighter escort, he was sending the Fleet south through the Canal 'to await events'.

Churchill could not conceal from Roosevelt his sense of shock. Forgetting his own role in the affair, he said later that 'defeat is one thing; disgrace is another'. Sympathetic as ever, the President asked what he could best do. The Prime Minister requested as many of the new Sherman tanks as possible. With amazing generosity towards his ally, Roosevelt relieved the US 2nd Armored Division, the first so equipped, of their 300 Shermans, with turret-mounted 75mm guns. To these he added 100 self-propelled guns of 105mm calibre.

Following its grievous succession of losses, the Royal Navy had been operating at a necessarily reduced tempo. It fell to the solitary *Eagle*, now repaired, to continue to bolster Malta's fighter defences. As Force 'H' was still absent in Indian Ocean waters, the old carrier was escorted by a scratch collection of equally elderly destroyers, mostly the splendid 'V&Ws'. Ten aircraft were lost owing to the fact that the launch position had to be located ever further westward because of the deteriorating situation in the Mediterranean. A third of the deliveries mentioned was timed to maximize available fighters in anticipation of the arrival of the next convoy. A creditable 95 were in fact estimated to be serviceable on the required date.

To divide the opposition's attention, it was proposed to sail a convoy simultaneously from either end. The Royal Navy had difficulty in adequately escorting both, and the Cyrenaican airfields were in Axis hands. The convoys were of unequal size, that from the west (Operation 'Harpoon') comprising six and that from the east ('Vigorous') eleven merchantmen. In the event of hard choices having to be made, 'Vigorous' would enjoy priority. Following normal practice, the 'Harpoon' convoy passed Gibraltar in the night of 11/12 June. A close escort of one old anti-aircraft cruiser (*Cairo*), five destroyers and four 'Hunts' would go all the way to Malta. A heavy force would cover the movement as far as the Central Narrows. This group comprised the battleship *Malaya*, the carriers *Eagle* and *Argus*, three cruisers and eight destroyers. Four fleet mine-sweepers and six motor launches (ML) fitted for sweeping were to accompany 'Harpoon' and precede it into Grand Harbour. To preserve fuel stocks on the island, a small Royal Fleet Auxiliary (RFA) tanker was to sail parallel to the convoy's course, refuelling the escorts as required.

Although shadowed by reconnaissance aircraft from early on the 13th, the convoy was not found by a first Italian air strike, operating at extreme range from Sardinia. A cruiser/destroyer force was sailed by the Italians from Cagliari but, though reported by British submarines already posted along its anticipated track, no attack on it could be mounted as it crossed to Palermo. It was not until the late forenoon of the 14th that 'Harpoon' suffered damage. Then, south of Sardinia, it was subjected to a co-ordinated high- and low-level attack. Torpedoes sank the Dutch freighter *Tanimba* and damaged the cruiser *Liverpool* sufficiently to oblige the latter to return to Gibraltar, robbing the convoy of two valuable destroyers for her escort.

Between 1820 and 2000 came an almost continuous assault by various combinations of aircraft. There were only 22 fighters all told on the two British carriers, and insufficient could be airborne at any time to cover all eventualities. Dusk saw the Gibraltar contingent turn back and the first long-range Beaufighters from Malta making a welcome appearance. With darkness, 'Harpoon' steered to pass close under Cape Bon, in the hope of staying inshore of the many minefields that now infested the Narrows. A lumpy sea frustrated an attempt at interception by three flotillas of Italian MAS boats but, ominously, the cruiser force sailed from Palermo.

Early on the 15th Beaufighters informed the Senior Officer of the escort, on board *Cairo*, that the Italian cruisers were closing from the north. They were duly sighted at 0620, just south of Pantellaria, and, as prearranged, the anti-aircraft escort stayed close aboard the convoy to make smoke while the destroyers made for the enemy. Before the destroyers could get within gun range, the Italians' heavier 6in were bringing them under heavy and accurate fire. Both *Bedouin* and *Partridge* were stopped by hits.

The Italian admiral, da Zara, endeavoured to work around to head off the convoy but ran into the smoke zone. As at Second Sirte, this proved a powerful deterrent to boldness, particularly as *Cairo* joined the destroyers in a belligerent defence. An Italian destroyer, *Vivaldi*, was temporarily immobilized, but the British had their hands too full to finish her off. Frustrated in his attempts to bypass the defence, da Zara gave up and, by 0930, had hauled off. As in Vian's earlier action, it was a close-run thing, for, at the end, every last 'Hunt' had also been committed to attack.

Once again, however, the enemy had succeeded in inflicting a decisive delay, and, still beyond Malta's short-range air cover, the convoy came under heavy dive-bomber attack. The American freighter *Chant* was sunk and the tanker *Kentucky* brought to a standstill. This valuable 9,300-tonner was taken in tow by the diminutive sweeper *Hebe*, causing the whole assembly to reduce speed to barely 6kts. This, of course, caused yet more delay, and a British ship, *Burdwan*, was severely damaged. The hard decision was made to abandon the two cripples and to push on at best speed with the pair of survivors.

Da Zara, having seen *Vivaldi* safely in tow, then unexpectedly came back. He fought off air attack from Malta and made for the three dense columns of smoke emanating from the abandoned merchantmen, whereupon his squadron wasted time in sinking them. *Hebe*, having slipped the *Kentucky*'s tow-line, had not yet caught up. Still in sight, she too was damaged by Italian fire, but she was able to give Captain Hardy of *Cairo* a warning of da Zara's return.

With just *Cairo* and three fleet destroyers, Hardy made for the Italians, but these had already pulled away. The British returned to their first priority, the convoy, while da Zara was able to deal at leisure with *Bedouin* and *Partridge*. The latter destroyer had managed to get under way again and was in the process of towing her still inert colleague towards the doubtful sanctuary of Tunisian coastal waters. The arrival of da Zara's squadron coincided with that of German and Italian aircraft. One of these torpedoed and finished the helpless *Bedouin*, but *Partridge* made good her escape.

Doggedly, the 'Harpoon' survivors forged on, now under a Malta-based air umbrella and reinforced by the minelayer *Welshman*, whose great range of attributes included a high-angle armament. Despite the precautions taken to counter mines, the aircraft-dropped influence variety outside Valletta defied countermeasures. Five ships, including one of the surviving two merchantmen, *Orari*, detonated them. Only one, the Polish-flag 'Hunt' class destroyer-escort *Kujawiak*, was sunk, but the repair of the remainder put a great additional strain on the heavily damaged dockyard. Between them, the *Orari* and the *Troilus* discharged 15,000 tons of mixed cargo but, as usual, the cost had been high.

Meanwhile Rear-Admiral Vian had been running the 'Vigorous' convoy from the Alexandria end. By borrowing heavily from the Eastern

Fleet, then forming in Ceylon, the escort had been boosted to five anti-aircraft cruisers, seventeen fleet destroyers and nine 'Hunts'. There were four 'Flower' class corvettes to augment the anti-submarine screen and two minesweepers to assist at the final hurdle. As a final *bonne bouche*, the ancient demilitarized battleship *Centurion* was present, fooling nobody with her disguise as a *King George V*. Submarines of both the 1st and 10th Flotillas were posted along all likely approach routes for Italian surface forces, and elaborate arrangements ensured that an aerial umbrella could be maintained for the greatest length of time. Finally, a newly arrived detachment of very long-range American Liberator bombers was stationed in the Delta, able to strike at any Italians from a considerable distance.

The existence of 'Vigorous' and its date of departure were disguised by dispatching ships individually from four separate ports. On 11 June (as the 'Harpoon' convoy approached the Gibraltar Strait) a preliminary detachment was sailed in the direction of Tobruk. It was designed to be seen, whereupon, its deception done, it would double back to join the remainder, which would sail two days later. The decoy group was indeed noted, and duly attacked by Crete-based Stukas, the *City of Calcutta* being damaged sufficiently to need to be sent into Tobruk. On 13 June the main junction was effected satisfactorily, but two ships, the Norwegian *Elizabeth Bakke* and the Dutch *Aagtekerk*, suffered mechanical breakdown and also had to drop out, the latter being sunk in sight of Tobruk.

During the afternoon of the 14th 'Vigorous' passed beyond the range of friendly fighter cover and soon lost the cargo ship *Bhutan* to bombing. At about the same time, the Italian Admiral Iachino left Taranto with both *Littorio*s, four cruisers and twelve destroyers. A Malta-based reconnaissance aircraft reported his strength precisely, a few hours later. Lacking any guns larger than those of his light cruisers, Vian queried of his C-in-C the wisdom of carrying on in the certainty of meeting two 15in battleships and four 8in cruisers the following morning (15 June). The chances of pulling off another Second Sirte appeared remote. Admiral Harwood responded enigmatically that Vian should hold his course until 0200 on the 15th, then reverse direction. This was apparently a device to get Iachino to advance to a point where he was vulnerable to aircraft and submarine attack.

Operating out of Derna, just two hours to the south of the point where Vian turned, were half a dozen units of the German 3rd S-Boat Flotilla. They struck as the convoy executed its tricky sixteen-point turn, hitting the cruiser *Newcastle* with a torpedo. Good damage control kept the ship operational, but the destroyer *Hasty* was not so lucky soon afterwards and was sunk. At this time, Iachino's squadron was about 200 miles north-west of the convoy and, at first light, itself underwent torpedo attack by Royal Air Force Beauforts. One of these reported having brought a 'battleship' to a halt, burning; she was in fact the heavy cruiser *Trento*. Leaving three destroyers to cover her, Iachino swept on.

Surprisingly, Vian was ordered by the C-in-C to reverse course again and head for Malta. The Italians, still closing, were undeterred by further air attack, in the course of which a Liberator hit *Littorio* with a heavy bomb, which exploded harmlessly on the roof of 'A' turret. This occurred shortly before 1000, at which juncture the stricken *Trento* was struck by two torpedoes from the submarine *Umbra*. A forward magazine exploded, sinking her within minutes.

Iachino was now under 150 miles distant, closing at a combined speed of better than 35kts. Harwood appeared torn between concern for the convoy and the desperate need to get it through. At 0940 Vian was again ordered to turn back, which he did. Then, soon afterwards, this directive was again countermanded. The experienced Vian, rather suspicious of the highly optimistic reports emanating from the pilots, believed correctly that he was heading for real trouble. In the best Nelsonian 'blind-eye' tradition, he ignored his final order and held on for Alexandria, his instincts being confirmed when Harwood gave him a free hand at 1420.

Aware of events, *Supermarina* then ordered Iachino to maintain his position, from which he could block any further attempt by Vian to get to Malta. This signal yet again prompted Harwood to change his mind: he suggested that Vian might get through with just the four fastest merchantmen. These ships, however, were under heavy air attack, losing the Australian destroyer *Nestor* and a 'Hunt'. Now very low on anti-aircraft ammunition, Vian continued on to Alexandria.

'Vigorous' was thus a failure, though *Littorio* was hit by a torpedo-carrying Wellington as Iachino returned—a success soon offset by the loss to a U-boat of the *Dido* class cruiser *Hermione* as Vian approached Alexandria. While only two of the seventeen merchantmen in the two operations actually arrived in Malta, the 15,000 tons discharged was little short of munificence to a population faced with starvation or capitulation.

Lord Gort, as Malta's Governor, began to receive the first hints of plans for a large-scale Allied landing in North Africa. His fighting instincts were quickly divided between using his meagre resources only in defence of the island and throwing everything at the Axis supply routes in order to weaken their military situation before any invasion. As things turned out, Malta was obliged to continue to defend itself. The faithful *Eagle* delivered 59 more Spitfires during July, but numbers of aircraft were now beginning to outstrip the fuel reserves and maintenance levels necessary to operate them at high pitch. Over a short period of intense combat, a quarter of Malta's 135 serviceable Spitfires were lost. In an effort to limit the growing strength of the island, the Axis sacrificed twice as many aircraft and, more importantly, their air crews. Air raids inevitably decreased in both size and number, and intruder raids by single fighter-bombers became more common. The minesweepers that arrived with 'Harpoon' made the approaches safe to a degree that enabled the 10th Flotilla submarines to return.

With splendid irony, the improvement in Malta's situation was offset by grave concerns for the fate of Alexandria: with the fall of Tobruk on 21 June, there was little to prevent Rommel sweeping on clear to the Delta. Morale plummeted as the Royal Navy dispersed ships to the north and to the south and prepared Alexandria for demolition. A particular loss, whilst en route to Haifa, was the 1st Submarine Flotilla's depot ship, *Medway*. Captain P. Ruck-Keene, the Flotilla Commander, was rescued from the sea and subsequently signalled the Admiralty: 'Regret to report *Medway* sunk by U-boat in position 31 deg. 3 min. North, 30 deg. 35 min. East. It was a beautifully executed attack'—which was the British habit of fair comment taken to its ultimate.

On Malta itself, Air Vice-Marshal K. R. Park relieved Lloyd as AOC: the latter joined the staff of Air Marshal Tedder, having seen the island's defences through a particularly trying time. Malta's invasion, Operation *'Herkules'* had been deferred, it will be recalled, until the DAK successfully took Tobruk, yet 23 June 1942, two days after that event, marked the point at which the operation was shelved indefinitely.

Detailed planning had been undertaken by a joint Italo-German team since the previous April. An Italian paratroop and airborne division were receiving intense training under German supervision. Six San Marco divisions, totalling 70,000 Marines, were prepared for the initial landings, and, in all, the 100,000 personnel earmarked for the assault would outnumber the defence by better than three to one. Five hundred special gliders were designed and built and a similar number of Ju 52 transports allocated: once Rommel's Tobruk objective had been attained, a further 500 Italian aircraft would also become available. Following heavy aerial bombardment, the planned airborne assault would be made on the high ground to the south-west of Valletta. This would not only dominate the capital but also make available the main airfields. A seaborne attack would secure Marsa Scirocco for use in the event of a large-scale rein-forcement by sea.

While high German circles still doubted the ability and commitment of the Italian forces, Kesselring pointed out the effect of malnutrition on the defenders and the fact that overwhelming air support would eliminate any local threat from the Royal Navy. Indeed, it has been reported that Lord Gort, on assuming the Governorship of Malta, brought with him not only the George Cross with which the protracted heroism of the Maltese had been recognized but also draft terms for surrender. Then, early in June, General Student, the airborne specialist, was summoned by the *Führer*. The latter was still convinced that German troops would be left in the lurch by their ally, and Student was forbidden to return to Italy. Admiral Raeder tried valiantly to get his leader to understand the continuing throttling effect that Malta was exerting on the campaign in North Africa and that only the complete removal of the nuisance by occupation would be effective in the long run.

If ever Hitler was swayed by these arguments, his opinion was certainly reversed by Rommel himself. Having secured Tobruk on the 21st, the jubilant Field Marshal found that the problem of his long logistics lines was solved for the time being by the vast quantities of stores taken as booty. He appealed directly to his leader to be allowed to continue a 'hot pursuit' of the Eighth Army into Egypt.

The *Führer* was entirely won over and wrote to Mussolini that they should not repeat the earlier mistakes of the British in North Africa: 'Fate, *Duce*, has presented us with an opportunity which will not occur a second time . . . it has always been my policy to pursue a beaten army to the utmost of our powers . . . I would beg of you one thing only: order operations for the total liquidation of the British forces to continue as far as your Supreme Command or Field Marshal Rommel can go with the forces at their disposal . . .' Mussolini, too, was seized with a vision of Egypt and the Canal, of gaining for Italy a fair share of the spoils. A triumphal entry into Cairo would go far to expunge the bitter taste of defeat in East Africa. Malta was effectively sidetracked. Rommel's promotion to Field Marshal affected the Axis command heirachy, so both Bastico and Cavellero were similarly elevated. Ciano noted sourly: 'Bastico's promotion will make the people laugh. Cavellero's will make them indignant.'

With Tobruk lost, General Ritchie gave it as his opinion that, with the resources available to him, a general withdrawal to the frontier was inevitable but, as that area was geographically unsuited to defence, it would be possible only to delay the DAK here until a proper defence could be organized on Mersa Matruh, a further 120 miles back. It was hoped that the hostile terrain between the border and Matruh would give the Axis forces problems that could be exploited to their disadvantage.

To General Gott, with a corps comprising four considerably under-strength divisions, fell the responsibility of fighting the delaying action, while two divisions under General Holmes frantically prepared the Matruh position. Beyond them again, a further 100 miles away, an additional corps under General Norrie would set up a further line. This was naturally strong in that, at its southern end, it terminated on the border of the Qattara Depression, a vast area of almost impassable soft going that made an outflanking manoeuvre virtually impossible. At the coast, some 35 miles distant, the new line would be anchored on an obscure railway halt called El Alamein.

General Auchinleck was in a quandary. The decisive battle was approaching—a battle that, if lost, would see the Axis occupy the Delta and the Middle East for, bar the Eighth Army, there was nothing to halt them. His protégé, Ritchie, could not be left to shoulder so heavy a responsibility. Not wishing to humiliate Ritchie by taking over himself, Auchinleck honourably wrote to the CIGS, offering his resignation and suggesting that, in his place, General Alexander should be appointed.

An immediate response from the Prime Minister expressed total confidence in the Commander-in-Chief, giving that extra resolution that enabled him to relieve Ritchie on 25 June. Churchill found repugnant the idea of voluntarily relinquishing a hundred miles of Egyptian soil and, despite the obvious military implications, called for a 'stern resistance' at the frontier. In this he was to be disappointed. To Auchinleck's military mind, the frontier was no more than an abstract feature in hundreds of miles of largely featureless desert. Probably influenced by his newly appointed adviser and personal staff officer, Maj-Gen E. Dorman-Smith, he abandoned even the idea of a set-piece action around Matruh. On 26 June he ordered the Army to prepare for a mobile battle between Matruh and the Alamein gap. It involved a style of warfare at which the DAK excelled but for which the Eighth Army was neither properly equipped nor adequately trained.

On 25 June Churchill and his War Cabinet were presented with a Vote of Censure placed in the House of Commons. Events in Europe and the Mediterranean were indeed proving painful, but were as nothing compared with the unrelieved run of disasters in the Far East. Powerful voices challenged the endless over-optimistic communiqués which made eventual truths the more unpalatable: poor generalship, which failed to match enemy standards and failed to exploit opportunity; inferior weaponry and armoured vehicles, upon which no remedial work appeared to have been undertaken despite adequate time and experience; the wrong aircraft, armed wrongly and used wrongly; a failure to harness British talent for inventiveness and ingenuity; and, predictably, why it was that, despite every effort at strangling his supply lines, Rommel was still waging a ruthlessly effective campaign. It says much for the British system that the Government could not only withstand such a withering blast of criticism but prove that the setbacks were the fault largely of earlier administrations and go on to trounce its detractors by 475 votes to 25. The exercise was, however, useful in that it reminded the leaders that Parliament and people did not possess unlimited reserves of patience for an extended war.

With the blessing of his High Command, Rommel hardly needed to check his stride before thundering on eastwards. Though well outnumbered in armour, he faced a demoralized opponent. By 23 June he was again east of the frontier wire, his advance sustained largely by captured vehicles, fuel and supplies. He had, however, also outstripped his air cover and was punished both day and night by a largely unopposed Royal Air Force. The rate at which Allied air power was growing was noted with concern, but it did not prevent the DAK from being within ten miles of Mersa Matruh by 26 June.

Two escarpments here ran parallel with each other and the coast. To their north and south Auchinleck had sited the bulk of his strength, but in the centre, on the plateau between the features, he placed two comparatively weak mobile columns. The C-in-C appeared to be inviting an attack in the centre, with the objective of nipping it out by counter-attacks from either wing. He had, however, made known his objective of keeping the Eighth Army intact. The result was ambiguity. Corps commanders had the options of fighting frontally, developing a flank attack to support their opposite number, or pulling out. Auchinleck's intention of fighting a mobile battle had also resulted in infantry being kept forward only on a scale determined by the transport available to carry them.

Delayed by air attack on his fuel supply columns, Rommel did not strike until the afternoon of 26 June. He attacked in the centre, even though he expected to meet the British armour there; this he rated sufficiently low that he expected to be able to punch through it with just 23 tanks and 600 motorized infantry. As might be expected, the DAK quickly brushed aside the British mobile columns once the protective minefields had been breached. Numerous calls for assistance convinced other commanders that the centre had been penetrated by a hundred panzers. Now, if ever, was the time to hit the DAK from either flank to cut off the advancing column. Instead, the bulk of the British armour remained inactive while each Corps commander passively awaited an attack in his sector before initiating a response.

While the advancing Germans were themselves tired and at reduced strength, they achieved much through their commander's boldness and natural flair for manoeuvre. Once through the central gap, his forces wheeled both north and south. To the north, with just 1,600 men reaching the coast, they convinced a whole British corps that it was cut off. To the south a New Zealand division thought likewise. Sheer panic, not assisted by the poor state of their communications, saw the British issue the code-word which initiated a general withdrawal to the Fuka Line, some 40 miles further east.

Ironically, the New Zealanders, who were uncommitted at this stage, found themselves withdrawing through the widely dispersed leaguers of the DAK. Clashes were unpredictable and fierce, Rommel admitting to 'very serious losses'. By 30 June the situation had stabilized again, but Mersa Matruh was now in Axis hands. Rommel had gained a significant victory through almost outrageous bluff—a victory that had cost his opponents 8,000 prisoners and a great deal of equipment. It was a terrible blow to morale.

The DAK was now less than 100 miles from Alexandria. It had covered 60 in the course of the battle for Matruh and there was every reason to think that it would take the city in a day or two. As the last of the Mediterranean Fleet evacuated the base, the sky above spewed a black snow—the fall-out from the incineration of countless classified documents. About the only hindrances left to the DAK were its own total exhaustion and the unchallenged attentions of the Royal Air Force, which bombed and strafed all that moved behind the known rear of Auchinleck's army. Once the latter established itself along the Alamein Line (still a geographical rather than a defensive feature), the C-in-C issued an Order of the Day. It stated that he believed himself to be heading an army that was in no way broken and that Rommel must not be allowed to seize Egypt by bluff. The painful truth had dawned that the Eighth Army had been bundled eastwards by a force deficient in just about every respect except generalship.

As two exhausted armies squared up to each other across the wilderness between Alamein and the Qattara Depression, political decisions were being taken that would have far-reaching effects on the campaign. It was seen as essential that a major effort be made in the West to relieve the enormous Axis pressure on the Russian Front. Powerful raids had been planned on either Brest or Cherbourg (Operation 'Sledgehammer'), but neither appeared to offer returns commensurate with the likely losses. A cross-channel operation ('Round-Up') was also being detailed by a UK-based group under Maj-Gen Dwight D. Eisenhower, but British resources earmarked for this had been drained by events in the Far East.

Despite a distinct lack of commitment from his principal military adviser, therefore, President Roosevelt agreed to Churchill's 'Super Gymnast'. By opening a new front in North Africa, the Allies would draw Axis forces from the East; then, once a victory had been achieved, the forces thus committed could be diverted elsewhere—i.e. Continental Europe. In the face of British opinion that 'Round-Up' could not be staged even in 1943, an operation in North Africa was agreed and, as 'Torch', it entered the detailed planning stage. It was to be mounted within four months, and on a scale sufficient to occupy French Morocco, Algeria and, if possible, Tunisia.

The Alamein Line, which stretched for nearly 40 miles from the coast to the elevated plateau that dropped steeply into the Great Sand Sea, featured the usual Western Desert terrain. For the most part hard, flat and totally monotonous, it was punctuated by the low ridges of Miteiriya, Ruweisat and Alam Halfa. Around Alamein was a fortified 'box' large enough to accommodate a division and a Corps Headquarters. In mid-gap lay an incomplete New Zealand box known as 'Kaponga', and also under construction was a third, on the edge of the hot, inhospitable plateau in the south; both these positions were designed to eventually accommodate a brigade. As the Eighth Army fell back and slowly reorganized, the garrisons of the boxes were brought up to strength and new positions began to plug the gaps between. Mobile groups also added to the strength in these sectors. Further to the east, a corps was devoted to preparing the Delta area for a last-ditch battle. Among its preparations were those for demolition and inundation, not the best ingredients for the restoration of morale in an army already accustomed to defeat and retreat. General Auchinleck's priority, however, was to keep this army in being, by whatever means necessary.

His forces already exhausted and depleted, Rommel could not engage in a major offensive, but he was convinced that his opponents should not be given time to regain their balance. If he could again place substantial forces in their rear, he considered that their defence would once more collapse. He was aware of his own parlous logistics situation but, totally unfairly, blamed this on the corruption, pomposity and over-organization of the Italian naval establishment. While, at higher levels, there was an element of truth in this assumption, it gave no credit for the dedication with which the supplies were continuously being fought across by convoys and combatants.

He knew also that the British were acting with uncharacteristic urgency—'Mortal danger,' he stated, 'is an effective antidote for fixed ideas'—and resolved to blast his forces through the line at a point between the Alamein box and the Ruweisat Ridge. By then again wheeling to both north and south, he would assault the boxes from their rear. What is certain is that Rommel was feeling increasingly vulnerable because of his deep advance and was well aware that, while the British were fielding American-supplied equipment in both quantitative and qualitative superiority, his own troops were now dependent almost entirely upon captured transport. To take the offensive now was the move of a hardened gambler. There could be no failure, but he could equally well not sit tight and await the inevitable offensive from Auchinleck.

Set an impossible timetable, Rommel's men were three hours late at their start line on 1 July. They were subjected to savage, round-the-clock air attack. Their intelligence regarding British dispositions and strength was sketchy. First the advance encountered an undetected strongpoint. Delayed, it was then heavily hit by fixed and mobile artillery fire. This barrage became so fierce that the thrust faltered, halted and began to fall back. Rommel, typically, tried in person to reach the critical area, but he found himself unable to. The British were using everything available, even lacerating the DAK with automatic anti-aircraft fire.

An attempt to remedy matters with a further effort that night proved abortive. Rommel ascribed the failure to powerful fixed defences but, in fact, he had been ensnared by Auchinleck's new mobile brigade-group strategy. His one success was the overrunning of the Indian brigade group at the initial strongpoint, but this had been achieved at the cost of eighteen of his slender strength of 55 tanks.

Unwilling to concede defeat, the German commander made a lunge at Kaponga but exposed his forces again to apparently unlimited barrage fire, now supplemented by a weak British armour attack. On 3 July a final throw was again defeated by remorseless artillery fire. In addition the Italian Ariete Division, which had begun to earn praise from Rommel, let itself down thoroughly in being badly worsted by the New Zealanders. The *Duce* himself had arrived in Derna on 29 June to prepare for a triumphant entry into Cairo. Talk was of Rommel being appointed Military Governor, with an Italian deputy. The First Battle of Alamein tempered optimism and, having done little for three weeks, the *Duce* flew home on 20 July.

German military staff in Rome were gloomy. Rommel's hard-driven divisions had each been reduced to between 1,200 and 1,500 fighting troops. There were 65 anti-tank guns left and, once again, just 55 tanks. 'Ultra' indicated that attempts to fly in troops from Crete drained the island's fuel stocks, so that sea transport had to be reverted to.

As the July heat lay heavy over the desert, an uneasy stalemate prevailed. The Axis simply had nothing left to give, while the British, for the moment, were content to have stopped moving backwards. Both sides, however, were building their strength. Many of the Italian troops who had been earmarked for '*Herkules*' were now transferred to the desert, but both they and German units were short of transport and heavy equipment. This was available in plenty on Italian quaysides, but in the Western Desert the Germans were now increasingly dependent not only on captured British transport but also on 25pdrs and ammunition. During the first six months of 1942, an average of 73,000 tons monthly was being landed by convoy, with a loss rate of only six per cent; now losses soared to over one-third of all material shipped.

General Auchinleck did not want things to stagnate, and he therefore decided to employ one of Rommel's own favourite strategies—a sudden shift of emphasis. A series of probes at the southern end of the line drew much of the available Axis armour to this sector. Auchinleck then had the New Zealanders and Indians pull out of Kaponga and the exposed southern box. These were occupied over the next twenty-four hours by the DAK, which, puzzled at the abrupt abandonment of defensible positions, were convinced that the British were withdrawing further.

On the morning of 10 July, however, the Italians in the northern sector were wakened by a concentrated artillery bombardment. It was the prelude to a thrust by Lt-Gen Morshead's seasoned 9th Australian Division, just transferred from Syria. The Italian Sabratha Division broke and retreated, abandoning most of its equipment. Only a resolute defence by an *ad hoc* German group prevented the Australians from punching clean through to menace the DAK's precarious supply lines. The DAK's Wireless Intercept Unit, which had proved so valuable, was caught in the volatile situation and destroyed.

Rommel, completely wrong-footed, quickly abandoned his intended plan, cobbled together an armoured battle group and threw it at the southern flank of the Australian salient. As his attack was only some 5,000yds from the massed artillery in the Alamein Box, it suffered badly and the front stabilized. Because it could neither penetrate nor outflank the Alamein Line, the DAK was unable to turn the battle into one of manoeuvre, where it would have an undoubted advantage. Instead it was being obliged to accept matters on British terms—slow-speed, set-piece infantry attack with local objectives. 'In static warfare,' Rommel observed glumly, 'victory goes to the side which can fire the more ammunition.'

On the 13th and 14th German armour, attempting to pinch out the salient, failed because the British artillery concentrated on the infantry following it up. With the limited enemy armour thus committed, Auchinleck had the Indians and New Zealanders move against the Italians along the line of the Ruweisat Ridge. Again the advance was halted only through the stubborn and quickly improvised German defence, but the success was marred by the high level of New Zealand casualties, caused mainly by poorly co-ordinated British armour support.

Rommel was by now alive to Auchinleck's tactic of hitting his weakest points and maintained a stability only through the rapid and continual deployment of his limited mobile reserves. Although the British C-in-C was now gradually winning a battle of attrition, time ran out. Churchill required him to defeat Rommel in short order so that much of the British resources could be switched to defending the northern access to the vital Middle Eastern oilfields. Auchinleck had to launch an offensive before 21 July, and he had just four days in which to plan it. In this battle ('Second Ruweisat'), the British intention was to assault the Axis centre, maintaining pressure until all the latter's reserves were commited before opening a second attack in the north along the Miteiriya Ridge, which feature formed a pivotal position in the DAK's defence. It had to work, for, like Rommel himself, Auchinleck had little in reserve.

During the night of 21/22 July the Indians moved along the axis of the Ruweisat under cover of a heavy barrage. Their advance was complemented by a scything sweep by the New Zealanders to the south. By daybreak on the 22nd the combined force held, as planned, a five-mile line, set normal to the ridge. It was desired to create a protected funnel through which the British armour could emerge, punch through the Axis armour concentration and power on westwards.

Unfortunately the 23rd Armoured Brigade was inexperienced and also equipped with outmoded 2pdr Valentines. They failed to penetrate a known mined area by dusk, leaving it until daylight on the 23rd. When they finally advanced, they ran at a fully alert opposition, their exuberant charge being first punished by more minefields and their covering artillery, then by a forceful counter-attack by the seasoned campaigners of the 21st Panzers. Ninety-seven Valentines left the start line, and 87 of them were lost. Again the infantry were left high and dry by deficiencies in British armoured strategy; again it was the New Zealanders who suffered most, and a certain amount of bitterness was engendered as a result.

Second Ruweisat had been a military disaster except in that it had diminished Rommel's resources to a point where he 'regarded the prospect of further British attacks with considerable disquiet'. He need not have worried, for the planned complementary thrust, westwards along the Miteiriya Ridge, was also poorly co-ordinated with its supporting armour. In collapsing, it saw more than a thousand troops, mostly British, made prisoner.

Again a hiatus settled on the arena. Auchinleck acknowledged that his resources were still inadequate and required further training, but he was apparently unaware of just how far his opponent had been worn down. Rommel was no longer planning an advance in the near future, relying on his battle-hardened 'Afrikaners' to buy time until adequate reinforcement arrived. At a time when he could have been particularly expected to rail against the qualities of his Italian allies, he was surprisingly generous in his appraisal of their average infantryman, who was 'willing, unselfish and a good comrade and, considering the conditions under which he served, had always given far better than the average'.

The German commander put the blame for Italian divisional failures at higher level—poor command, poor training and poor equipment. The Italian soldier was supported by weak artillery and worse armour and, as he begged food from his German comrades, his officers, for the most part, 'refused adamantly to forego their several-course meals'.

In the three months to the close of these July battles, the Germans claimed to have taken 60,000 prisoners and to have destroyed over 2,000 armoured vehicles. These are sad statistics indeed, but Auchinleck had succeeded in his primary aim: he had prevented the DAK from reaching the Delta. His enemy had also suffered significantly, and now both sides rebuilt and re-trained, knowing full well that the next offensive by either would likely prove decisive.

NINE

The Turning of the Tide

August 1942 to November 1942

AS TWO ARMIES glowered across the Alamein Line, like a pair of exhausted boxers who longed for the final bell but who each coveted the trophy too much to give in, the struggle to save Malta went on. Viable numbers of defending Spitfires had caused the withdrawal of the hated but vulnerable Stukas. In their place were versatile Ju 88s, which still required fighter cover. The Me 109s comprising this were also obliged to look to their own defence. Air Vice-Marshal Park brought his experience as a Group Controller in the Battle of Britain. Radar and vectored fighters not only combined to break up potential raiding formations at long range but also took the war to enemy airfields on Sicily .

From the third week in July 1942 the island had the threat of invasion lifted indefinitely as forces trained for '*Herkules*' were transferred in large numbers to reinforce Rommel's impoverished army. Neither the population nor the garrison was aware of this, of course, and all still faced defeat from sheer privation. With the Government-regulated diet already reduced to only two-thirds of the nutritional value of standard rations in the United Kingdom, all livestock was compulsorily purchased for slaughter and distribution. The provision of this once-only windfall of protein also freed grazing land for crops. It was against these grim and deteriorating conditions that the next relief (Operation 'Pedestal') was planned: as, simply, the 'August Convoy', it was to secure a place in history.

By Mediterranean standards, 'Pedestal''s thirteen cargo ships and one tanker constituted a large convoy, for the first time including ships that were both American-owned and American-manned. Long daylight hours had necessitated the suspension of Arctic convoys for the summer mmonths, enabling the Home Fleet to buttress Vice-Admiral Syfret's covering forces to a level previously unheard of. In addition to the 16in battleships *Nelson* and *Rodney*, the Admiralty had put together a force of three carriers, the veteran *Eagle* being supported by the modern *Indomitable* and *Victorious*. Between them they carried 72 fighters and 28 torpedo aircraft. Also in company was the old *Furious*, with a load of 38

Spitfires for Malta. Each carrier had a *Dido* class anti-aircraft cruiser assigned as 'goalkeeper', and there were thirteen destroyers and two 'Hunts'. Together these comprised Force 'Z', which was to proceed no further than the Central Narrows. To take the convoy right through was Rear-Admiral Burrough's Force 'X', which included three modern 6in cruisers, an elderly 'C' class conversion, seven destroyers and four 'Hunts'. Eight older destroyers were also attached, both to escort *Furious* and to cover any casualties. Finally there were oilers and an ocean tug, all covered by their own corvettes.

On Malta, the strength had been built up to nearly 200 aircraft. 'Pedestal' was to be forced through, but so massive an effort was bound to generate an equally massive response. This was to be confused by the running of a 'spoof' convoy from Alexandria and deliberate coat-trailing by submarines. However, while security lapses advertised 'Pedestal' well in advance, the Italians were unable to operate any of their four battleships because of an acute shortage of fuel. Though the Germans themselves needed to be economic with oil, it is difficult to explain their starving of the Italian Navy. This service was the key to their success in North Africa—at once the means of escorting Axis convoys and hindering those of the British.

Thorough preparations were, nonetheless, made to prevent the passage of the 'Pedestal' convoy. These were aimed at progressively weakening the convoy, reducing its capacity for self-defence until, during the last lap, it could be brought to action by surface units and destroyed. Even though the airfields in French North Africa could not be used, the Axis air forces assembled the better part of 1,000 aircraft on Sardinia and Sicily. A series of temporary minefields was laid by the Italians, and twenty submarines were deployed over the convoy's likely track.

Passing eastward through the Gibraltar Strait in the early hours of 10 August, 'Pedestal' was favoured by thick weather, only to run into a fleet of Spanish fishing craft. Thus reported, it then encountered its first submarine, the Italian *Uarsciek*, before dawn on the 11th. She claimed to have sunk *Furious*, but no enemy activity was noticed by the escort until 0815, when the corvette *Coltsfoot* reported two porpoising torpedoes passing at a safe distance.

Despite the attentions of carrier fighters, reconnaissance aircraft now stuck with the convoy. *Furious* was able, about midday, to commence flying off her Spitfires, Malta still being nearly 600 miles distant. Attention was suddenly diverted as *Eagle* was struck by a torpedo. Even as a score of binoculars were trained on her she was hit again, then twice more, all on her port side. She slewed to a stop, adopting a rapid list and trailing an immense wall of multi-hued smoke. As the convoy ploughed resolutely on, the stricken vessel heeled further, the sight unreal on a brilliant afternoon and in a calm, sparkling sea. Eight minutes later she had passed into history, leaving only a dispersing pall and 900 survivors struggling in oil-covered water. The culprit had been Rosenbaum's *U73*, which had evaded seven destroyers (whose asdic/sonar had been smothered by the sound of the convoy and water noise) and then passed beneath the whole assembly. *Furious* pulled out urgently the moment the last Spitfire had left had deck and, on passage back to Gibraltar, evened matters slightly when the destroyer *Wolverine* of her escort rammed and sank the Italian submarine *Dagabur*.

An air attack commenced in failing light at 2045 on the 11th. A mix of Ju 88 bombers and He 111 torpedo bombers were successfully engaged by fighters and guns, losing several of their number to no avail. British and American aircraft bombed Sicilian airfields during the night in the hope of causing disruption.

A diversion was the sailing from Malta on 10 August of the *Orari* and the *Troilus*, the two 'Harpoon' survivors. Hugging the coast in darkness under Cape Bon, they and their two destroyers ran into a small Italian force engaged in minelaying. Gunfire was exchanged, but neither side pushed for a decision as each was intent on its primary task and mindful of the fact that the unidentified opposition could well prove to be Vichy French.

On 12 August events opened with a strike by nineteen Ju 88s, which achieved nothing for the loss of six of their number. This attack, however, had been only a dress rehearsal. The main turn, commencing about midday, involved a mix of over 100 aircraft. For ninety minutes the convoy manoeuvred as best it could, hitting back with all at its disposal, including the firing of 16in guns at low elevation to raise walls of water to deter torpedo-droppers. Italian circling torpedoes caused interesting diversions but no damage. Considering the quantities of explosive being expended, it was extraordinary that there was only one casualty. The Blue Funneller *Deucalion*, her shell-plating ruptured by a series of near-misses, trimmed quickly by the head and was obliged to drop out. She headed for the Tunisian coast but was caught again and finished off by an air-dropped torpedo.

At about 1345 the assault terminated in something of a *tour de force* by two Italian Re 2001 fighter-bombers. Their unfamiliar silhouette enabled them to overfly *Victorious* without being brought under fire. One hit the carrier with its single heavy bomb, but from so low an altitude that it did not arm. It ricocheted from the armoured flight deck without exploding. Two hours later the convoy, nearing Galita Island off the North African coast, ran into the main concentration of Italian submarines. The destroyer *Ithuriel* flushed *Cobalto*, finishing her off by ramming. Her commanding officer described the impact as a 'delightful crunch' but damaged his stem

takeover by either side, and, in the event of *force majeure*, to scuttle itself. From the Allied point of view, a major cause for concern regarding French intentions was the agreement by Laval to cede to the Axis 150 French-flag merchantmen, whose 650,000 gross tons would go far to offset losses on the North African convoy route.

On 23 November the events of this confused period took a further turn when the French military base at Dakar, complete with the naval units located there for the duration, joined the Allies. It had been strongly anglophobic since the abortive Operation 'Menace' of September 1940 and its change of mind was symptomatic of the times. The timing was unfortunate in that it was influential in the German decision to move against Toulon.

Plan 'Anton' saw German troops first seize the high ground dominating either side of the entrance to Toulon. After so much notice, it seems strange that they were able to effect a degree of surprise in the very early hours of 27 November. Although quickly on full alert, the Fleet had no steam with which to move. By 0530 German tanks were clattering over the dockyard cobbles and de Laborde, from his flagship, the battleship *Strasbourg*, gave the order to scuttle. This was to be no matter of simply putting the ships on the bottom in shallow water. Every vessel had charges in each major turret and in vital machinery such as gearboxes.

French crews took considerable risks to blow the charges, and frantic scenes developed as they jostled on the brows to get ashore, even as German troops pushed to get aboard. Magazines and torpedoes began to explode and the sky over Toulon darkened as oil fires took hold. Only four submarines succeeded in breaking out, to be interned in Spain. Shortly after Dunkirk the French had given the British a solemn undertaking that their Fleet would never be allowed to fall into enemy hands. At Toulon on that dark day in November they honoured their commitment to the letter. From this proud Fleet the Italians were able to raise and repair only four destroyers; the remaining ships were wrecked beyond repair.

On 10 November the French ceasefire ordered by Admiral Darlan appeared to be the 'green light' for Allied armies to stream eastwards to catch Rommel between two fires. It promised to be something of a walkover, but the promise proved to be stillborn.

Hitler received the news of 'Torch' with a degree of enthusiasm. Convinced that it would cause the French to join the Axis, he offered to 'protect' the North African territories. His representatives were well received by senior French officers in Tunis, of whom Admiral Esteva ranked immediately below Admiral de Laborde. Discussions with Laval in Munich then resulted in Tunisian airfields being placed at the Axis' disposal and a military build-up began in earnest. Within the week the newly appointed *Fliegerführer Tunisie* could muster over 80 fighters, mostly Me 109Gs but including a dozen of the new Focke Wulf FW 190s. These were tasked with covering the flow of aerial transport and also missions of the available 30 Stukas. The job of the latter was to begin the daunting task of holding back the inevitable Allied advance.

By the end of November nearly 17,000 troops had been flown across to form the nucleus of the new German 90th Corps, formally constituted on 16 November. It was commanded by General Walter Nehring, who was still recovering from wounds received at Alam Halfa. Though his task was considerable, Nehring had on his side an exceptionally mountainous terrain with a limited range of communications, which greatly favoured a resolute defence. He also gauged correctly that Bizerta and Tunis would be the primary Allied objectives, and that the Allies would probably also thrust south-eastwards to reach the coast on the Gulf of Gabes, a move which would split the Axis forces and threaten Tripoli. He acted with foresight and decision and, soon reinforced by a fresh panzer division, settled down to make an eastward Allied advance as expensive as possible.

ELEVEN

The Road to Tunis

November 1942 to March 1943

EVENTS IN NORTH AFRICA from November 1942 tend to overshadow activities at sea. Malta, nonetheless, remained the key to the success or otherwise of the Axis in resupplying its armies. The island remained a beleaguered outpost in a hostile sea, its privations eased but not terminated by the high-profile success of 'Pedestal', the August convoy. As matters stood, even with small parcels of stores delivered by submarine and fast minelayer, Malta could survive little longer than mid-November without a further convoy.

Since the Germans' disastrously incorrect decision to defer the 'final' assault on the island until after Rommel's success in Egypt, it had recovered somewhat as a base for assaults on the Axis convoy routes. Over each of the final six months of the year the Italians delivered an adequate 56,000 tons. However, this statistic disguises the fact that this was less than two-thirds of the total being dispatched. The remainder, together with an average 55,000 gross tons of shipping, was being destroyed en route.

Under pressure to assist, Kesselring responded with another 'mini-blitz'. Waves of Spitfires, directed by radar, intercepted his raiders even over Sicily, so that each *Luftwaffe* bomber had to be covered by up to seven fighter escorts. Pitched battles ensued, with the Germans pushing through resolutely to cause some damage. In the course of the nine days' offensive, the Royal Air Force lost 32 Spitfires; their opponents lost twice this number of aircraft, together with their air crews. As *Furious* then brought in a new batch of fighters, the Germans could see that they were getting nowhere and gave up, falling back on the old standby of incursions by single fighter-bombers. It is worth recording that this operation by *Furious* (Operation 'Train' of 29 October 1942) was the last such to ferry fighters to Malta. Including *Wasp*'s two contributions, a total of 28 runs had been made, delivering 719 aircraft. Without them, Malta could not have hoped to survive.

After Alamein, Montgomery's advance quickly secured airstrips as far west as Gazala, enabling air cover to be given for much of the passage of a westbound convoy. This, Operation 'Stoneage', comprised four merchant ships, two American, one Dutch and one British, which passed non-stop into the Mediterranean via the Suez Canal. Its progress was monitored by a newly established joint operations room and the escort reflected the major danger posed by air attack. Although the Italian Fleet could still muster six battleships, the chance of surface attack from this source was virtually discounted. In the event, appreciations proved to be accurate and, except for a single bomb hit on the cruiser *Arethusa*, 'Stoneage' arrived unscathed on 20 November. It was followed a fortnight later by 'Portcullis', comprising five freighters and a tanker. These two operations ran 56,000 tons of supplies and, with their virtually unchallenged deliveries, they can be said to mark the point at which Malta's long siege was finally lifted. Pairs of freighters subsequently ran every few days.

Malta's build-up enabled a challenge to be mounted against the free use by the Axis of the short sea route between Sicily and Tunisia. Although the Central Narrows here are not above 60 miles in width, the distance between the significant ports of Palermo and Tunis/Bizerta, complicated by a chequerboard of minefields, was above 150.

Captain Simpson's 10th Submarine Flotilla had been making a thorough nuisance of itself on the convoy routes throughout October, and this was one reason for Kesselring's mini-blitz. 'Ultra' information, confirmed by aerial reconnaissance, warned of sailings from Naples or Palermo, enabling submarines to be pre-positioned. Such a warning saw five boats located suitably in mid-October, to intercept a group of three freighters and a tanker, covered by eight destroyers. They were duly sighted by *Utmost* on 19 October, some 40 miles north of Pantellaria. Her sighting report resulted in an attack by *Unbending*, which sank the 4,500-ton *Beppe* and a large destroyer. An attempt by *Unbroken* was not successful, the submarine being quite severely shaken from the accurate depth-charging to which she was later subjected. A Malta-based FAA aircraft torpedoed the tanker, *Petrarca*, a further torpedo being added by *United*. Tankers are tough, however, and, though disabled, *Petrarca* was towed to Tobruk. Just before daylight on the 20th *Safari* scored the final success by rounding two escorts and disposing of the 5,400-ton *Titania*.

With the continuing inactivity of the fuel-starved major units of the Italian Fleet, only the Royal Navy's submarines could really see much action. On the day following 'Torch', *Saracen* caught and sank the Italian submarine *Granito* as it cruised on the surface near Trapani. 'Tubby' Linton's *Turbulent* sank the U-boat supply ship *Benghazi* off Sardinia; she took with her most of the Germans' stock of electric torpedoes.

A few miles from the spot where *Granito* was destroyed, *Unruffled* shot the bows off the new 41kt light cruiser *Attilio Regolo*. The Italian vessel had to date conducted only a single minelaying sortie and now had to spend six months in dock. One tragic result of this unrestricted warfare was the sinking of *Scilla*. She was carrying over 800 British prisoners of war, only about two dozen of whom survived.

Though losing over 60 aircraft during November, the *Luftwaffe* stuck doggedly at its task of building up German military strength in Tunisia. Perturbed, the British moved eastwards from Algiers without air cover having first been established. On 11 November a brigade was landed, unopposed, at the port of Bougie, some 130 miles further east. A further operation, to seize the nearby airfield of Djidjelli, was aborted because of heavy surf. Enemy aircraft, with no fighter defence to contend with, found easy pickings offshore. Three valuable liners, *Cathay*, *Karanja* and *Awatea*, aggregating over 38,000 gross tons, were destroyed, along with the anti-aircraft ship *Tynwald*, lately a Liverpool–Isle of Man packet. The big 15in monitor *Roberts* was heavily hit and immobilized, which enforced her absence from the next 'hop' to Bône, a further 100 miles to the east. As Spitfires were operating from Djidjelli by 13 November, this move was carried out with deceptive ease by two companies of Commandos, transported in a brace of 'Hunts'. At neither Bougie nor Bône had the French offered resistance, but U-boats now became a problem, sinking the Blue Funneller *Maron* and Lamport and Holt's *Browning*.

These losses were acceptable in that the capture of Bône had an immense psychological effect on the Italians. Already having had to open up a new convoy route, to Tunisia, on diminishing resources, they now found routes vulnerable from the west as well as from Malta, to the east. They nonetheless succeeded in shipping over 30,000 tons of supplies and several thousand personnel by the end of the month. Their occupation of Corsica at this time was a hollow success, disguising a growing realization of pending disaster in North Africa. Mussolini had been thwarted by the scuttling of his 'share' of the French Fleet, though its acquisition without the bunker fuel on which to run it would have had propaganda value only. In contrast, the Allied Fleet had been reinforced with the new battleship *Richelieu* from Dakar, three cruisers, three 'super-destroyers', three flotilla destroyers and seventeen submarines.

On Christmas Eve 1942, in a final twist to the endless agony of French loyalties, Admiral Darlan was assassinated. While his true allegiancies remain mysterious, his authority in North Africa was of extreme value to the Allies. The very ambiguity of his public persona led to his shooting by a 'patriot'.

A great assembly of aircraft, together with their ground organizations, moved on to the crowded airfields of Malta. The 8th Submarine Flotilla and its depot ship moved forward to Algiers and MTBs to Bône. Force

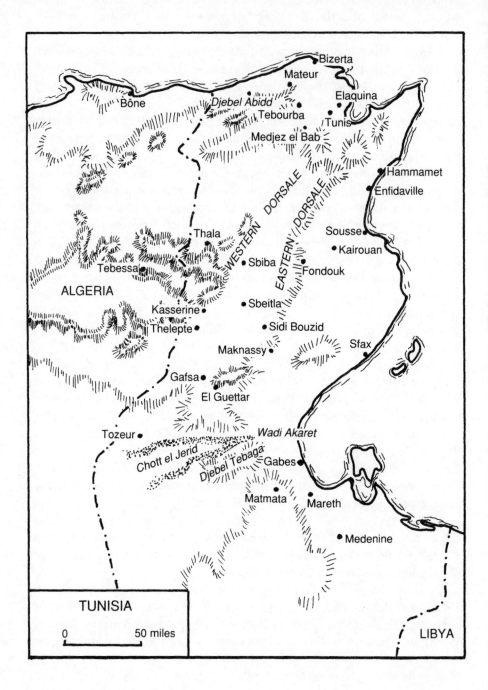

Bizerta
Mateur
Bône
Djebel Abidd
Elaquina
Tebourba
Tunis
Medjez el Bab
Hammamet
Enfidaville
WESTERN DORSALE
EASTERN DORSALE
Thala
Sousse
Sbiba
Kairouan
Tebessa
Fondouk
ALGERIA
Kasserine
Sbeitla
Thelepte
Sidi Bouzid
Maknassy
Sfax
Gafsa
El Guettar
Tozeur
Wadi Akaret
Chott el Jerid
Gabes
Djebel Tebaga
Matmata
Mareth
Medenine

TUNISIA

0   50 miles

LIBYA

'K' was reconstituted with three *Dido*s and four destroyers; based on Bône was Force 'Q', with three light cruisers and a pair of destroyers. The latter, in a midnight battle near the Skerki Bank, sank a complete Italian convoy of four ships, together with one of its destroyer escorts; a second was towed home, half her complement dead. This operation was marred only by the loss on the following morning of the destroyer *Quentin*, which fell victim to a German torpedo bomber. A two-ship convoy was destroyed during the same night near the Kerkennnah Bank.

Two days later, on 4 December, American heavy bombers hit the dockyard at Naples. Still being repaired from submarine torpedo damage incurred the previous August, the cruiser *Muzio Attendolo* was destroyed. Two other cruisers and four destroyers received varying degrees of damage. The result was that all except one cruiser division, based at Messina, were moved north and west to La Spezia and Maddalena. Even without its chronic fuel problems, the Italian Fleet was now virtually without a capacity for intervention where it mattered. For a period, until extra mine barriers could be laid, the Italians resorted to running single ships by day, each vessel protected by a massive aerial umbrella.

The coast continued to be hazardous for British ships. Enemy submarines sank the destroyer *Partridge* and blew her sister *Porcupine* in two. Both halves of the latter were towed in but were never reunited. They became semi-permanent features, known, inevitably, as 'Pork' and 'Pine'. The 'Hunt' class *Blean* was sunk and the fast minelayer *Manxman* damaged. A torpedo salvo from the Italian boat *Mocenigo* hit the cruiser *Argonaut*, simultaneously removing either end. As the cruiser's outboard shafts still turned, she reached port and, eventually, the United States for complete repair. The destroyer *Ithuriel* was bombed beyond repair and the two valuable passenger liners *Strathallan* and *Cameronia* destroyed. On 12 December three cargo ships were sunk and two damaged at Algiers by 'human torpedoes' and combat swimmers delivered by the Italian submarine *Ambra*.

On 14 November 1942 the British First Army began to move overland from Bône, the nature of the terrain suiting only brigade-size formations. The advance was cautious and along two main axes. Contact was made with French troops under General Barré. These were in divisional strength but were scattered and lacked heavy weapons. They held several key locations but were reluctant to give the British all-out support as the latter were still apparently at low strength, far outnumbered by the very obvious German presence. For a time the French resisted German probes, but when it became apparent that Allied help was not yet available, they fell back.

General Anderson's planned assault on the city of Tunis by 22 November proved to be a pipedream. Working from all-weather airfields near the capital, the *Luftwaffe* was far more effective than the Allied air forces at close ground support, also harassing minor Royal Navy units which were engaged in running military supplies to any suitable point along the coast. Allied air support organization was still skeletal, and the availability rate dropped off alarmingly. Supported by American armour and artillery, General Anderson's troops moved in the direction of Tunis itself on 25 November. The advance was along three axes, but each front was severely constrained in width by the terrain. Encounters with the enemy thus tended to be on a relatively small scale but were fierce by the nature of their concentration.

Bold probes by American armour, notably one that captured Djedeida airfield, complete with a score of Stukas, persuaded General Nehring to pull back somewhat to shorten his defensive line. With Tebourba and Djedeida taken by 27 November, Allied troops were within a dozen miles of the capital. Here General Anderson halted, swayed by an appeal from one of his Divisional commanders, Maj-Gen Evelegh, to observe a pause until the Royal Air Force could exert some sort of brake on the rampant activities of the *Luftwaffe*. The halt was unfortunate, coinciding with the arrival of Field Marshal Kesselring. He chided Nehring on his caution and directed him to throw all available armour at Tebourba. This, including the first 88mm-armed 'Tigers', scored a notable psychological victory in retaking the town and its area, along with 1,000 prisoners, 50 tanks and much equipment.

Anderson and Evelegh appeared depressed by the general level of enemy activity and argued that they were overextended. Any resumption of the advance on Tunis, planned for 9 December, they made dependent upon the availability of further resources and an improvement in the balance of air power. Uncertainty was rife. Supported by Anderson, one of his Corps commanders, Lt-Gen C. W. Allfry, wished to make a tactical withdrawal. This was vetoed by Eisenhower, who roundly criticized activities in Tunisia as 'violating every recognized principle of war'.

Kesselring was quick to see the difficulties faced by the Allies and his own advantages in defence. Having made a comprehensive case that the situation was ripe for exploitation, the Field Marshal received a full headquarters organization, with his forces being regularized as the 5th Panzer Army. As such, it got a new commander in Col-Gen Jurgen von Arnim.

With only half the resources of the Allies, the Germans suffered little disadvantage as the terrain permitted only limited numbers to come into contact. Consolidating their hold on Tebourba, they were thus able, with a force of just 30 tanks, to penetrate fifteen miles along the valley of the Medjerda. A resolute French battery brought them to a halt just short of the strategic location of Medjez-el-Bab.

Incessant winter rains put rivers in spate, turned over-used roads into tracks and made tracks into quagmires. Fighting stagnated; morale deteriorated. Anderson's pause, due to end on 9 December, was extended to the 16th, then to the 24th. Then, on Christmas Eve, Eisenhower was obliged to back Anderson in abandoning the thrust on Tunis and going on to the defensive. Axis reinforcements moved in steadily, but where this made the conquest a more formidable prospect, it was at the cost of military strength in Sicily and southern Italy. Moreover, every man added to German or Italian forces in North Africa increased further the supply problem across a wide and unfriendly sea.

General von Arnim's situation was far healthier than that of Rommel. Fortunately for the latter, the pursuing Eighth Army still exhibited an ennui, a mixture of fatigue and anti-climax following a major battle, and shortages of transport and fuel. Attempts at looping around the retreating *Panzerarmee* failed first at El Daba, then at Fuka. Much of the Axis army was on foot, but every attempt by its more fortunate motorized elements to halt and allow them to catch up was thwarted by the dogged tailing of the British armour, which kept them moving.

Montgomery, since Alamein a full General, was now certain that his army would see no more 'serious fighting' until it reached Agheila. This position exhibited much of the natural strength of Alamein but it lay about 750 miles away, and the British held all the cards. Why Montgomery, with his ideals of the *corps de chasse*, could contemplate such a prolonged retreat by his opponent without bringing him to action is not clear. Instead, he lists his tasks as being to capture and secure the Agheila position against any further incursions from the west, to station a corps 'strong in armour' in the Djebel Akhdar to take in the flank any Axis force that was successful in penetrating eastwards and, finally, to create a powerful Royal Air Force presence in the Derna and Benghazi areas to provide close air support on demand.

On 6 and 7 November it rained. It rained so hard that three British divisions were bogged down and almost out of fuel. Rommel's situation was no better, since, while two-thirds of his command had succeeded in reaching the next planned halt, a road junction south-west of Mersa Matruh known to the British as 'Charing Cross', a whole panzer division, fuel-less, was leaguered still only half way from Fuka. As fuel columns could not get through to them, the vehicles had to be destroyed and the crews evacuated as best as possible in trucks. The metalled coast road was the key to any progress by the *Panzerarmee*. While it was hampered by congestion, movement was possible. The Eighth Army, attempting to outflank it across the open desert, was halted almost entirely by bogged-down wheeled transport, upon which it depended. Waterlogged airstrips and low cloud-bases also prevented the Royal Air Force from punishing the retreating enemy columns. Near Fuka the remaining 6,000 troops of the Italian X Corps were captured virtually complete. Within ten days, 17,000 Italians had been taken prisoner, causing the British extra logistic problems until they could be shipped to the rear.

It was as Rommel moved westwards out of Matruh during the night of 7/8 November that he learned of 'Torch'. He had planned a further delaying action at Sidi Barrani, about 70 miles further on, in order to allow his motorized forces time to get through the bottleneck of the Halfaya Pass. Here a 25-mile jam formed quickly, attracting air attack and preventing the movement of essential supplies from the rear. The Field Marshal himself supervised the clearance of this chaos, his sense of urgency increased by the knowledge that two Eighth Army divisions were outflanking the location.

More prisoners and equipment had now been taken by the British than remained to their opponents, and Mussolini belatedly began to be concerned for the remaining Italian units. To protect Tripolitania it was necessary to buy time in which the Agheila Line could be strengthened. Although the combat zone was still over 300 miles to the east, the abandonment of Cyrenaica was already assumed. Rommel was, therefore, ordered to fight a delaying action on the line Halfaya–Sollum–Sidi Omar, on the Egypt/Libya border. The order was an empty one. On 9 November a total of 5,000 Germans and 2,500 Italians, a score of tanks and perhaps 100 guns faced a fully mechanized and armoured army of three full-strength corps. Even at night British aircraft worried at the Axis columns, by the almost continuous light of flares. As the *Panzerarmee* fell back past Capuzzo, the British entered Sollum and occupied Halfaya.

Rommel's request that Kesselring and Cavellero come and discuss the overall situation in North Africa was turned down, and the emissary that he then sent to the *Führer*'s headquarters was informed brusquely that the Field Marshal should assume that Tunisia would be held and that he, in turn, should maintain a grip on the Agheila/Mersa el Brega position at all costs.

Just one day after the British entered Sollum, their leading elements were 100 miles further on, entering Tobruk without opposition. Without command of the sea there was no way in which the Axis could contemplate leaving an isolated garrison, and two regiments of armoured cars, moving towards Acroma, had been sufficient to convince them that they were about to be cut off. Needing about 250 tons of fuel daily to maintain an orderly retreat, the *Panzerarmee* was getting only about 200, most of it by courtesy of an overtaxed *Luftwaffe*. Its vehicles were, in any case, slowly diminishing in number as mechanical failure and air attack took their toll. Rommel again noted on 15 November that his pursuers were content to keep things moving rather than seek battle. The assessment was accurate as Montgomery's strategy was 'to take no chances'.

Four British columns, hindered by demolitions, fuel shortages and the weather, maintained the westward momentum both sides and across the Djebel Akhdar, the high ground that formed the spine of the Cyrenaican bulge. One was probing at Msus when news reached Rommel of a sizeable British movement by sea. With 'Torch' very much on his mind, the commander assumed it to be an amphibious thrust against Benghazi. It was, in fact, the 'Stoneage' convoy, which had left Alexandria on 18 November. It was sufficient to trigger a large-scale destruction of stores and irreplaceable fuel and the demolition of port installations. In the event, the British did not arrive—overland—until the 20th.

Three Malta-based aircraft sank the large tanker *Giulio Giodani* off Misurata on the 18th, which gave the *Panzerarmee* one last fuel scare before it retreated, still in good order, behind the Agheila defences during the night of 23/24 November. Twice before the Axis had used this position as a springboard to launch their forces on a wild dash eastwards. Montgomery was determined not to allow this to be repeated. He had advanced 700 miles in a fortnight, and his own logistics were creaking ominously, but his aim was to bundle his opponent from Agheila without delay.

The Royal Navy cleared Tobruk and Benghazi and got them working by the 20th and 26th respectively. Army engineers rapidly refurbished the railway extension to Belhamed. Worn-out transport was run to a standstill, but the supplies kept coming. Montgomery's gaze was on Tripoli, the ultimate prize, still some 550 miles beyond Agheila. About half way between them ran a second defensive line, anchored on Buerat.

Now located at the psychologically important gateway to Tripolitania, the Italians worked hard to improve the Agheila position. Rommel arrived on the 24th and told them that the British would simply outflank them. The ground to their south was very difficult—saltmarsh, soft sand and broken wadi—but it was passable. The Field Marshal therefore dispatched to Rome General de Stefanis, one of the few Italian senior officers for whom he had respect. His task was to convince the High Command that three infantry divisions, without adequate transport, would simply be a liability and, almost certainly, lost. Ironically, given adequate strength, Rommel would probably have counter-attacked at this juncture as the British advance forces were very weak, ripe for picking off before they could fall back on their main body.

On 24 November Rommel met Kesselring, Cavellero, Bastico and von Rintelen at the Arco dei Fileni. This edifice, known to the British as 'Marble Arch', straddled the Via Balbia at a point some 40 miles east of Agheila, on the frontier between the provinces of Cyrenaica and

Tripolitania. Rommel proposed to move out instantly without waiting for the British to move up unassailable strength. To stay would require a massive resupply of equipment and fuel—an impossible condition now that Hitler had granted priority to Tunisia. Dictators, however, are not swayed by military logic, and Mussolini reiterated—no retreat from Agheila. 'Extremely indignant,' the Field Marshal went on the 28th to Hitler's headquarters to put his case. The *Führer* flew into one of his uncontrollable rages, virtually accusing the *Panzerarmee* of bringing its troubles upon itself. Rommel departed, 'angry and resentful'.

Rommel, the realist, was thinking in terms of vacating not only the Agheila Line but also Buerat and even Tripoli itself. With the odds that now faced him, his opinion was that the first location that stood any chance of being defended successfully was Gabes, just inside the Tunisian border and 600 miles distant. Hitler, like Mussolini, had decreed that there be no retreat from Agheila and had put *Reichsmarschall* Göring himself in charge of providing the means of defence. He and Rommel visited the *Duce* in Rome and, while Göring's general manner made him few friends, Rommel succeeded in conveying to Mussolini the gravity of the situation, discussing with him the best means of pulling the Italian divisions to Buerat.

Montgomery was in absolutely no hurry, and the Axis forces watched, fascinated, as the British underwent a massive reorganization (in the course of which a complete corps lost its identity) and a new military juggernaut took shape. Such was the air of inevitability that Rommel moved first and began to move his forces back during the night of 6/7 December, a decision that consumed much of his remaining fuel and transport. He did not need to rush, for the British commander had set the date for his attack as 15 December and left his deputies to continue preparations while he returned to Cairo to visit Alexander and to purchase some new kit.

For the while the Germans were occupied in coping with incessant air attack and aggressive British patrolling. The positions that they held were strong enough to convince the British commander that the time-honoured outflanking move to the south was again the best option. A full five days before the main offensive broke, therefore, General Freyberg and his New Zealanders were dispatched on a looping 200-mile trek, over extremely difficult ground, with the objective of cutting off the enemy by reaching the coast near 'Marble Arch'. Their advance could scarcely go unnoticed and, once reported by aerial reconnaissance, confirmed Rommel's doubts. He began his withdrawal in good time, skilfully delaying the 51st (Highland) Division and the 7th Armoured Division that sought to bring him to battle. In the event, when Freyberg reached the sea near Merduna, it was to see the last of the *Panzerarmee* escaping westwards along the

Via Balbia. It had escaped the trap, and what Montgomery termed the Battle of Agheila was, in reality, no battle at all. Spoils were few and poor weather hindered flying.

Rommel's fuel situation influenced his every movement. He claimed that nine supply ships out of ten were sunk at this time; the tenth carried no fuel. His retreating motor transport columns consumed 95 per cent of what he had. More was lost through its deliberate targeting by the Long Range Desert Group (LRDG), regarded by the German commander as a major nuisance.

The *Panzerarmee* moved into the Buerat position over Christmas, again untroubled by Montgomery who, now that Agheila was safely behind him, settled back for another build-up. This was to generate sufficient power to advance all the way to Tripoli in one thrust, it being already a point of honour that the Eighth Army, not Anderson's First, should be the means of taking the enemy's most vital port.

It was now Allied convoys that were discharging at Tobruk and Benghazi, with 3,000 tons crossing their quays daily by the end of December. In contrast, 87 Italian ships, grossing 12,800 tons, were destroyed during the last two months of the year. As 1943 dawned, the Axis' situation in North Africa was looking increasingly precarious. While the Royal Navy kept their seaborne supplies to an insufficiency, their military forces were being compressed relentlessly from east and west. British submarines were extremely active, taking fearful risks in waters now sown with thousands of mines, laid by friend and foe alike. Nonetheless, of the five lost in the Mediterranean during November and December, three were victims of surface escorts, while of the two possibly mined, one was sunk off Sardinia and the other off Taranto.

The *Duce* became depressed about the possible loss of Tripoli and its effect of the people's will to continue the struggle. Forgetting his recent 'realistic' discussions with Rommel, he began to complain bitterly about plans to retreat in good time and to call for a Stalingrad-type defence of the town. Again the German commander had to plead with his ally to face facts, observing that 'the length of our stay in Tripolitania will be decided by Montgomery and not by *Comando Supremo* . . .' Marshal Bastico was able finally to convince his High Command, who then agreed to an Italian infantry withdrawal only on the understanding that Rommel held on to the Buerat position for six weeks.

As the Eighth Army grew menacingly in strength, so the *Panzerarmee* weakened. During the first week of 1943 alone, 30 tons of ammunition arrived to replace the fifty tons expended, 800 tons of fuel to replace 1,900 tons. Unable to sustain all of his strength, Rommel moved the 21st Panzer Division to cover the Gabes defile, starting on the 13th. It showed Rommel's lack of commitment to Buerat, but it would also guard against a thrust from the west by Eisenhower's forces. As the unit could also be supplied from Tunisia, the move eased logistic problems.

Despite violent January storms which reduced Benghazi's throughput to nearly zero, Montgomery began his offensive to time on 15 January. His aim was to cover the 200 miles to Tripoli within ten days. He also hoped to bring his opponent to action; Rommel, facing annihilation, was not prepared to oblige. Following a still cautious advance, under continuous air cover, British forces entered Homs, 65 miles short of Tripoli, on 19 January. To the south-west, an armoured column reached Tarhuna. Although the Axis had planned a stand on a line between the two towns, the immediate threat of outflanking again occasioned a withdrawal. Rommel was only delaying the British advance, and by 20 January he was within earshot of the explosions that marked the demolition of the port of Tripoli.

Only a few miles from the town, the ultimate goal that it had slogged all the way from Egypt to secure, the Eighth Army was suddenly seized by an acute shortage of transport. All available was, therefore, given to a single corps, which drove on to Tripoli along three simultaneous axes. On 23 January 1942, three months and 1,400 miles from its start line at Alamein, the Eighth Army entered Tripoli unopposed. Though there were growing voices in the Italian High Command calling for Rommel's replacement, the Field Marshal had kept his army intact and was, even now, using it to fortify the Gabes area, in what came to be known as the Mareth Line.

On 15 January the Italian freighter *d'Annunzio* had left Tripoli, escorted by a single torpedo boat, *Perseo*. As with so many of her predecessors, she was found by Malta's reconnaissance aircraft and intercepted and sunk by Force 'K' destroyers. She was interesting in being the last survivor of the 883 convoys sent by the Italians to Libya. Nearly 1.3 million gross tons had been lost—342 ships, representing 60 per cent of available capacity in the Mediterranean at the opening of hostilities. About 2.25 million tons of supplies and fuel had been shipped, of which 86 per cent had been delivered. By any standard, the Italian Navy and mercantile marine had succeeded in their aim, and they had succeeded through persistence and dogged courage. Five cargo ships, grossing 25,000 tons, were scuttled in Tripoli harbour, too damaged to be worth recovery. From this point only submarines and small auxiliary craft could use the port, and from 23 January even these were unable to do so.

To underline their dominance in North Africa, the Allied leaders staged a major conference at Casablanca in January 1943. General de Gaulle, however, attended only after much prevarication on his part. He had no wish to meet Giraud on an official platform, thus publicly recognizing him. Having declined several invitations to attend, he received a withering telegram from the British Premier. It concluded: 'The position of His Majesty's Government towards your Movement while you remain at its head will also require to be reviewed. If with your eyes open you reject this unique opportunity we shall endeavour to get on as well as we can without you . . .' He attended.

Among the far-reaching decisions made at Casablanca was the ambitious aim of defeating Germany by the end of the year. In the Mediterranean, Sicily would be the next objective, its capture opening up the sea to Allied shipping and, effectively, releasing 200 standard-size merchantmen. The Americans still believed that the quickest way to defeat Germany was to take the war to German soil, but, however laudable this aim, they had to be convinced that the means simply did not exist at this time. Sicily invaded would pull more Axis strength from the Eastern Front, would hasten the fall of Mussolini and would encourage Turkey to declare for the Allied cause.

A major *faux pas* at the Conference was President Roosevelt's declaration that the enemy powers would be made eventually to surrender unconditionally. It caught the mood of the time and soon gained wide currency, but, despite later efforts by both the President and the Premier to water it down, it has been held subsequently to have prolonged the final stages of the war. In the near term, however, North Africa still had to be recovered.

Three days after the British entered Tripoli, a sick and disillusioned Rommel was informed by *Comando Supremo* that the 'German-Italian Panzer Army' was to pass under the command of the Italian General Messe once it arrived on the Mareth Line. Rommel's state of health was given as the reason, but, without doubt, his unorthodoxy had made him more than a few enemies in OKW. Triumphant, he remained unassailable, but now, in defeat, the jackals closed in.

It was, in any case, a time of great changes in the Axis High Command. Messe, complaining that his appointment was no more than a means by which Cavellero could get rid of him, had the satisfaction of seeing the latter being replaced by General Vittorio Ambrosio as Chief of Staff of the Italian Armed Forces. Cavellero was deemed to be too 'pro-German'—an interesting comment on relations between the partners. Subordinate to Messe, Col-Gen von Arnim took command of both German armies in Tunisia, now combined as 'Army Group Africa'.

This left Bastico with little function and, as with the loss of Libya his governorship had lapsed, he too departed the stage. Von Arnim answered in practice to Kesselring. Each was looking over his shoulder at events in Stalingrad, where the German Sixth Army, once 22 divisions strong, was about to capitulate. It required very little imagination to see that a parallel situation could well develop in Tunisia.

A final move affecting the war in the Mediterranean was that occasioned by the resignation of Admiral Raeder. Following a decidedly lacklustre performance by his Fleet off the North Cape on the last day of 1942, its head received a tirade from the *Führer*. Hitler proposed to decommission all heavy units; Raeder objected, was overridden and resigned. His place was taken by Admiral Dönitz, whose submarines were active in the theatre.

On 2 February 2 1943 Messe arrived to find that Rommel had decided to stay on. This, of course, was entirely against orders and, for a month until he finally left, it resulted in a highly confused chain of command. Rommel had found the Mareth Line to comprise no more than a system of antiquated and demilitarized French-built blockhouses, fronted by broken country, wadi and saltmarsh. It was commanded by high ground to the east, the direction from which Montgomery could be expected to come. Armour could attack the line in places and, while difficult, outflanking was possible. A second line was, therefore, prepared at Wadi Akarit, which could be defended by non-motorized infantry. It was, however, 40 miles beyond Mareth and, remembering that Eisenhower's forces were but 75 miles from dividing the Axis forces in two, 40 miles was a lot to consider yielding.

With Anderson still stationary before Tunis, General Eisenhower was, indeed, planning just this. His proposal, however, was scotched by the British, who forecast that the completely untried Americans would be trounced by the veterans of the *Afrika Korps*. While Eisenhower then deliberated on how best to keep the pressure on his opponent, Rommel struck. In his usual bold manner, the latter calculated that he could get in a quick initial blow against the Americans and defeat them before the Eighth Army could intervene from the east.

The Allied line followed roughly the axis of the so-called Eastern Dorsale, a north–south chain of low mountains that rose in places to about 3,000ft. Kesselring recognized the strategic value of the passes through this barrier and directed von Arnim to secure them. The centre of the line was held by a French corps. To the north of this force were the British, and it was at the corps boundary that the enemy attacked. Code-named '*Eilbote*', the operation was designed to roll up the French sector from north to south while the British were held back by the newly arrived 10th Panzer Division.

As the Germans had suspected, the French, with no recent battle experience, gave ground. The going, following weeks of rain, was glutinous, and even the ponderous Allied command system was able to shift assets quickly enough to bring the thrust to a halt. A rude shock had, however, been administered, not least by the taking of 4,000 Allied prisoners. The bulk of the French were pulled out of the line for re-training and re-equipping, and the American Maj-Gen Fredendall was placed in command of all Allied troops in the south. His response was ineffective when, almost immediately, the veteran 21st Panzers grabbed the valuable Faid Pass.

Hints abounded of a projected large-scale Axis attack timed for mid-February, but, as it was to be all-German, radio traffic was minimal and hard facts difficult to garner. Von Arnim and Rommel were at loggerheads: each had his own scheme and each required the better part of the three weak panzer divisions available. In the event, Kesselring flew over to settle the dispute, but he achieved only an unsatisfactory compromise which put Rommel in the supporting role.

The operation ('*Frühlingswind*') was to open with the 10th Panzers bursting through the Faid Pass. They were to link with the 21st, which would loop around from the south, the combined force heading off north-westward. Rommel, with what was essentially still his DAK, would stage a feint along the Gafsa–Kasserine road, the axis that he, in any case, felt was strategically more important. The 170 tanks involved included five of the new Mk VI 'Tigers' and about fifty uprated Mk IV 'Specials'.

Breaking on 14 February, the offensive soon marooned the local American garrison on the high ground that it was defending. The latter's artillery-led defence was hampered considerably by a concentrated *Luftwaffe* effort. This resulted in the American defenders of Gafsa being rushed northward to assist. Rommel was thus able to coast into Gafsa on the 15th without resistance. Covered by von Arnim's activities, the DAK moved further, its commander apparently aiming to proceed via the Kasserine Pass to take the important centre of Tebessa. From this location he could probably influence the Allies to pull back considerably.

Having achieved their initial objectives, the German forces now appeared to run out of ideas, the terrain somewhat dangerously dividing their advance into three separate axes. Once again it was Rommel who saw how to exploit the situation, and he requested the transfer of von Arnim's armour to assist. Only on the 19th could these be prised from the latter's group (though he retained a significant force, including the Mk VIs). Being considerably scattered, the armour did not reach Kasserine until the 20th, by which time the DAK, and the Italian Centauro Division in support, had moved on. In this they were assisted by the low level of Allied air activity, due to the continuing foul weather.

Defending doggedly, the Americans repulsed the Germans' first attempt to take the Pass, but the latter, bringing up the 10th Panzers, succeeded so rapidly that the Americans were obliged to abandon much equipment. Its quantity and quality both impressed and sobered Rommel when he inspected it. As directed by *Comando Supremo*, the advance then turned northwards in the direction of Thala and Le Kef, overriding

Rommel's opinion that Tebessa was the more important. The Americans adopted the strategy of holding the high ground, their trained observers calling down artillery concentrations of 'astounding flexibility and accuracy' on the German columns, which were restricted to the valley bottoms. With neither time nor resources to dispute control of the ridges, the latter steadily incurred casualties, their advance slowing as it plunged ever deeper into hostile territory. To avoid their ultimate and inevitable loss, Rommel and Kesselring met early on 22 February and agreed a withdrawal. By the following day all Axis units were once again east of the Kasserine Pass and Rommel's priority became one of getting back to the Mareth Line quickly enough to defend it against a move by Montgomery.

The Allied command structure had once more proved unequal to the task. Kesselring rated the fighting ability of the Americans as poor and proposed further exploitation. Rommel, however, was more cautious, noting their lavish levels of supply. Once this was married to battle experience, they would, he felt, be difficult to defeat. In any case, his own talents for fluid, manoeuvre warfare were severely offset by the nature of the Tunisian terrain. He had long preached the ideal of force concentration, yet at Kasserine he had been made to participate in a battle where strength was dissipated over 40 miles of mountainous terrain, with three separate forces which were not mutually supportive. In material terms the Axis were clear winners, but, as the Allies could replace equipment almost immediately, this was of little consequence. Ground lost was quickly recovered and, as the battle revealed weaknesses in the command chain which were also rectified, the Allies gained by the experience.

The German thrust could, in any case, have been little more than a foray as the same forces were required also to cover Mareth, and an over-ambitious advance would certainly have been nipped out and destroyed totally once improving weather allowed Allied air power again to be brought to bear. It had, nevertheless, achieved its objective in badly shaking the inexperienced troops that had faced it. So large had these forces now grown that, on 20 February, they had been redesignated the 18th Army Group, under the command of General Alexander, who acted also as Deputy Commander-in-Chief. On the 22nd, before the problems of Kasserine had been resolved, Alexander reported to Churchill and the CIGS in damning terms. He was 'frankly shocked' by the situation, the 'real fault [being] lack of direction from above from [the] very beginning, resulting in no policy and no plan'.

Army Group Africa, the German equivalent, came into being on 23 February. Kesselring put Rommel in command rather than von Arnim, due to the latter's obstructive and negative attitude during 'Frühlings-

wind'. Rivalry still persisted, however, and, while Rommel readied for a spoiling attack to disrupt Montgomery's planned move against Mareth, von Arnim was successful in persuading Kesselring of the merits of his own operation. This, code-named '*Ochsenkopf*', comprised a series of co-ordinated thrusts spread over 50 miles of the northern end of the front. Opening on 26 February, it started well, pushing back the green troops of the British 46th Division.

Further south, an armoured thrust by about 80 tanks saw nineteen of the vaunted Tigers go into action. These were the vehicles that von Arnim had held back earlier. Penetrating toward Beja along a narrow defile, and hindered by the rain-softened going, the force ran into a well-sited British anti-tank block. No fewer than fifteen of the Mk VIs were included within the total of 71 tanks disabled in the débâcle. This severe reverse was offset by the Germans' holding the field and recovering 49 of the casualties for eventual repair.

Rommel was disgusted when he heard of this result, but his dislike of von Arnim was such that it is possible to detect a note of pleasure in his account of the latter's discomfiture. Even so, the end was clearly nigh. The 46th pulled itself together, and within five weeks of the launch of '*Ochsenkopf*' it had recovered the territory that it had lost. Two major Axis onslaughts had now expended themselves with no permanent gains: neither had caused the Allies more than local embarrassment, while irreplaceable resources had been expended.

His health severely undermined and his morale down to an all-time low, Rommel prepared for his assault on Montgomery's assembly areas near Medenine. His pessimistic outlook was shared by General Warlimont, the Deputy Chief of the Operations Staff at OKW, who was in Tunisia to acquaint himself at first hand with the situation. He reported that less than half of the army's supply needs were now being met, yet, despite this, he forecast that, at the current rate of loss, no suitable supply ships would remain by 'June or July'. Action then in progress around Kasserine was castigated as 'ill-advised' and the whole Tunisian set-up as 'a house of cards'.

Fuel remained a major problem, with both of February's shipments being intercepted and sunk. Malta-based aircraft made a sustained and ultimately successful effort against the ex-Norwegian *Thorsheim*, while, on the same day (the 21st), the submarine *Unruffled* accounted for the *Baalbek*. A parallel and crippling loss was that of the *Utilitas*, off Palermo. Downed by a submarine, *Turbulent*, she was transporting 5,000 tons of bunker fuel—reportedly half the stocks available at that time to the whole Italian Navy.

Army Group Africa was now compressed to the extent that it needed to switch its resources from one front to the other as circumstances dictated.

This it did effectively enough in difficult circumstances, and it does Montgomery no credit that he records having Rommel 'running about like a wet hen'. In fact, the former was obliged to use Eighth Army resources on a diversionary attack, the effect of which was to delay his main task.

Details of Rommel's move against Medenine were known to the British, via 'Ultra', by 1 March. While all three panzer divisions were known to be committed, it was computed that these now amounted, in total, to no more than 31,000 men and 135 tanks. Montgomery's staff worked furiously to ready the army by the specified date. Reinforcements in armour and infantry were sited at the expected point of attack. On call were 350 field guns and 460 anti-tank guns (including 3.7in heavy anti-aircraft guns parallelling the German 88mm in low-trajectory fire). At the expense of mines for static defence, plenty of ammunition was brought forward. There were also about 300 tanks. The ground had been prepared intelligently, the Axis forces (under the tactical lead of General Messe) being encouraged to expend their energy fruitlessly against strong positions. In front, camouflaged, was the bulk of the anti-tank guns, sited to take the enemy armour in enfilade. Close behind were the infantry, dug-in and invisible on reverse slopes. Armour was kept back for use in counter-attack as the situation required.

It was to be the gunner's day. Appearing uncertain as they advanced through an early ground mist, the panzers were allowed to approach to within a few hundred yards before the concealed guns gave tongue. The infantry were given a free spectacle as each enemy probe was beaten back. Under Rommel's eye the armour persisted, with mounting losses. Only along the line of the shallow Wadi Hallouf did they make any ground and there, after 27 tanks had been already destroyed, a group of Shermans engaged them from static positions. This was the only British armour to be involved.

At about 1700 Rommel, as Army Group Commander, gave the order to withdraw. Messe had achieved nothing and left behind the wrecks of a third of his slender armoured strength. At virtually no cost in casualties, the British had won the Battle of Medenine with 30,000 rounds of anti-tank ammunition. A depressed Rommel, acknowledging that his attack had been a week too late and had inconvenienced Montgomery not one jot, wrote: 'A great gloom settled over us all'. Again, however, he had fared better than he thought because Allied aircraft were for the most part grounded by the weather. It was obvious that the Axis forces were no longer sufficient to cover the 400 miles of their two fronts. As these could be pierced almost anywhere by superior Allied pressure, Rommel suggested to his High Command that ground be relinquished in order to shorten the fronts to a more manageable 100 miles. Indeed, he went further in requesting to know the High Command's long-term intentions for the defence of Tunisia, querying his forces' very presence in North Africa.

Informed by Kesselring that his *Führer* was 'unable to agree [his] judgement of the situation', Rommel resolved to confer with him directly in an effort to save the veterans whom he had led across the see-saw battlefields of North Africa. He handed over to von Arnim and flew out to Rome on 9 March 1943. He was never to return.

TWELVE

The End in North Africa

March 1943 to May 1943

FIELD MARSHAL ROMMEL stopped off in Rome to confer with General Ambrosio, the new Italian Chief of Staff. He was surprised to discover that he could expect to be placed on sick leave, pending a new appointment. A meeting with Mussolini followed. To Rommel's dismay, the *Duce* seemed to 'lack any sense of reality', being concerned primarily with the effect that the loss of North Africa would have on public opinion. He offered a further division of troops, in response to which Rommel had to explain that it was more important to equip properly those that were already there.

On proposing the shortening of the front line, Rommel was called 'defeatist'. He learned later that the conversation had cost him the planned award of the *Medaglia d'Oro*, Italy's highest military decoration. He then met Hitler, who, deeply depressed at the Stalingrad disaster, labelled Rommel's plan 'pessimistic'. The only Tunisian territory to be yielded was to be that involved in the shift from the Mareth Line to that of the stronger position at Gabes. Rommel was, however, invested with the Knight's Cross, with Oak Leaves, Swords and Diamonds, the senior German award. Disillusioned nonetheless, he headed off to commence his sick leave, with von Arnim confirmed as his successor.

General Alexander took rapid steps to improve the fighting qualities of his raw troops. Fredendall was replaced by Patton, and the Eighth Army was robbed of seasoned NCOs to man newly established battle schools. Few escaped the rigours of courses at these, the crash programme making up time squandered by Anderson and, to a degree, by Eisenhower.

General Montgomery did not, as might have been expected, go on to attack the Mareth position while his opponent was still shaken by the defeat at Medenine but spent a fortnight in preparation. He had little faith in the abilities of the Americans, his attitude sowing seeds of antipathy which would flourish and affect later relationships. He suggested to Alexander that Patton's men advance through Tebessa to seize Gabes, mounting a show of force to threaten the Wadi Akarit Line from the rear. They were to create dumps which would permit the Eighth Army, once past Mareth, to press on through the Gabes Gap and to retain momentum to sweep the enemy from his final bastion. Patton disagreed. He believed that the best training was battle experience and was prepared to take losses to prove it. He had four divisions, 90,000 men and no shortage of confidence. The Axis forces that opposed him were of only a quarter this strength.

The Mareth Line spanned the 20-mile gap between the Matmata Hills and the sea. Its obsolete fortifications had now been strengthened and equipped with modern weapons. Beyond lay the further chokepoint of the Gabes Gap, which was fortified along the natural obstacle of the Wadi Akarit. This barrier stretched fourteen miles between a vast saltmarsh and the coast. General von Arnim expected the Eighth Army to punch through Mareth near to its seaward end, then to turn and roll the line up.

Montgomery, however, knew of a pre-war French study which had confirmed a feasible route for several divisions, capable of outflanking Mareth by the landward side of the Matmata Hills. He had the LRDG re-survey the track and, once the suitability of the route was confirmed, instructed General Freyberg to take 27,000 of his New Zealanders and 200 tanks along it. Setting off on 10 March, Freyberg was in place to the west of the hills a week later. He had, however, been observed by the enemy. Mareth still had to be breached and, though defended by greatly understrength units, 70 per cent Italian, the line remained formidable. As its immediate mobile reserve it boasted the 15th Panzer Division—now just 32 serviceable tanks strong.

Opening during the night of 16/17 March, the assault on Mareth was triple-headed. Inland, the Americans' thrust (with the typically Patton-esque label of Operation 'Wop') took Gafsa and, in pouring rain, headed on for Maknassy. In the centre a Guards Brigade attacked a strongly held eminence known as 'The Horseshoe'. Their task had been compromised by captured documents and the brigade incurred over 500 casualties in overcoming the thoroughly prepared defence. The survivors held the hill briefly but were so reduced in numbers that they had to be evacuated.

Near the coast two British divisions pushed the Italian defenders back to the line of the Wadi Zigzaou, maintaining the pressure in order to draw the enemy reserves. During the night of 20/21 March a major crossing was attempted, but the wadi was so soft that only three tanks could make it. Until the next night this toehold on the far side was defended furiously. During darkness, supreme efforts by engineers allowed forty Valentines to get over before the whole ford became an impossible quagmire. It was unfortunate that these tanks were early models, with only 2pdr guns. Without the backing of 6pdr anti-tank guns, which could not cross, they suffered badly at the hands of the numerically inferior 15th Panzers, losing 30 of their number. The pocket was all but eliminated.

Making a virtue of a necessity, Montgomery put this part of the line on to the defensive and sent a further armoured division to reinforce Freyberg. As this required three days in which to catch up, Montgomery was obliged to request Patton to stage a diversion. This he supplemented by sending an Indian division along the line of the difficult Matmata Hills, threatening the inland end of the Mareth Line.

By 20 March Freyberg was poised to take the strategically important Tebaga Gap, from which the port of Gabes and the cutting off of the Mareth Line were but a short step. Probably due to his British Army training, Freyberg was not willing to send his armour through the Gap by night. The hiatus proved critical for, by the morning, the Germans had plugged it with two divisions, one of them armoured.

Patton had duly obliged Montgomery and, on 23 March, his forward elements occupied a gap at the small settlement of El Guettar. German armour succeeded in infiltrating their positions, and the situation was looking slightly precarious when they ran into an American defensive minefield, losing 38 vehicles. The remainder withdrew and the defenders, now in excellent spirits, were able to repulse a later, follow-up attack supported by heavy dive-bombing.

With El Guettar now firmly held, Alexander had the Americans quickly funnel through an armoured division to threaten and unbalance the defenders of the Tebaga Gap. The attack on this feature was still, however, to be undertaken by Freyberg's New Zealand Corps. Known as 'Supercharge II', it was to open on 26 March and was unusual in several respects.

During the previous night over 400 tons of bombs were unloaded over the enemy's forward positions, while the attackers moved forward to their start line. They then had to stay concealed for twelve long hours, their attack being timed deliberately for 1600 so that they would come in with a lowering sun at their backs. Half an hour before the 'off', a further saturation bombing strike hit the defenders, who emerged, disbelieving, as a tide of khaki flooded in from the pall of dust. Attacking at this time of the day was not a British habit. With waves of aircraft roaring in at head-height and shooting up anything that moved beyond the advancing infantry, objectives were quickly taken. By 1800 the 1st Armoured Division had moved up and halted at its pre-planned location to await darkness.

A full moon rose at about 2300, as obliging as the sun before it, and the armour rolled on. This, of course, was also decidedly unusual and would have succeeded had not a parallel series of dry wadis lain across the line of advance. By night, these proved to be a substantial obstacle, slowing the advance sufficiently to allow the Germans to improvise an anti-tank screen. While this did not check the British thrust, it delayed it further, winning time just sufficient for General Messe to pull his forces back from the Mareth Line and quickly through the Gabes Gap. The task for the British was to hit the defences of the Wadi Akarit before the Axis troops could settle.

An attempt on 28/29 March by two American armoured divisions to tackle Messe from the western flank was frustrated by determined opposition from the 21st Panzers, backed by a full-scale *Luftwaffe* onslaught, directed personally by Kesselring. It was apparent that the Germans were now rating the Americans more highly, and it assisted the Eighth Army greatly to have them draw off some of the more experienced defenders. In fairness, however, they were not over-pleased with being used in what they saw as a continuing supporting and 'spoiling' role. Even without being defeated militarily, however, Messe's army would be obliged to fall back, owing to the deteriorating supply situation—a fact well apparent to the Axis High Command.

Algiers, Bône and Bougie, though being heavily and persistently attacked by the *Luftwaffe*, were packed with shipping. Stores and ammunition, vehicles, armour, artillery and personnel poured over their wharves in an unending round-the-clock stream. In contrast, Bizerta and Tunis, the only significant ports remaining to the Axis, were working to only half their already reduced capacity. The reason, quite simply, was that the flow of shipping was at last drying up.

Italian convoys now faced almost insuperable odds. Submarines roamed to the very threshold of their assembly ports. Allied air power was not only in greater strength and operating from ever-nearer airfields, but was also being augmented by heavy bombers, such as Liberators, which were able to range well to the north of Sicily. Torpedo aircraft and surface units awaited anything in range of Malta. An atmosphere of helplessness and inevitability was engendered by the almost inevitable sighting by reconnaissance aircraft (although the role that 'Ultra' played in this remained unknown).

The available Italian and German tonnage was, by now, largely dissipated. New construction was totally inadequate, and recent French 'windfall' tonnage was mostly run down from disuse and required thorough refit, the capacity for which did not exist. To help meet the shortfall, the Germans used the French inland waterways system to move to the theatre considerable numbers of small, prefabricated craft. These, the so-called Siebel ferries and F-lighters (more correctly *Marine-Fahrprahme*, or MFP) could stow typically a dozen vehicles or about 150 deadweight tons of cargo. Artillery in transit was always ready for use, and this, together with the fact that their draught was too shallow to enable torpedoes to be activated, often made the craft formidable adversaries for Allied light forces.

Comando Supremo still aimed to ship 80,000 tons per month, supplemented possibly by a further 10,000 tons brought by air. In total, however, this was only half of their army's needs. Many Italian fishing vessels were, therefore, pressed into service. These were not only ill-suited to the task but were better employed in providing a vital part of the nation's food. As usual, a fleet turned to its destroyers. Each could accommodate 300 troops on the seven-hour sprint across the Narrows and, amazingly, 52,000 Axis troops were thus transported in this phase. Resources for those men already there would have been more appropriate. Opinion in the Royal Navy, which itself had sacrificed so much to support campaigns ashore, acknowledged the Italians' achievement. Admiral Cunningham was particularly generous in his praise of their courage and persistence.

At sea, torpedo-armed Beauforts now operated alongside American B-25 Mitchell and B-26 Marauder medium bombers, escorted adequately by long-range P-38s. High-value targets were often carpet-bombed, even before they sailed, by formations of up to eighteen B-17s, each with a three-ton payload. Based at Algiers, with their depot ship *Maidstone*, were the submarines of the 8th Flotilla. Old, unsuitable boats had by now all been replaced by modern units of the 'S', 'T' and 'U' classes. Current strength was six 'Ss' nine 'Ts' (one of them Dutch-manned and flagged) and three 'Us', a mix of craft that allowed boats to be matched with specific patrol areas.

Dangers in the submariners' world had not in any way lessened, and three 'T-boats' went missing in March 1943 alone. Probably awaiting a troop convoy off Pozzuoli, *Tigris* was lost on a mine. Off Sicily, the torpedo boat *Cicogna* accounted for *Thunderbolt*, which had started her career as the unfortunate *Thetis*. Then, on the 23rd, came the loss of *Turbulent*. She was cornered in shallow water off the Corsican coast when her skipper, Cdr J. W. 'Tubby' Linton, was typically pressing home an attack. As a tribute to his record, Linton was awarded a posthumous Victoria Cross.

Perversely, surface strike forces were not enjoying the best of success. Where submarines could lurk unseen at choke-points, and aircraft had the speed to respond rapidly, ships reacted usually to information received. If action were joined at night, advantages such as superior firepower and even radar were offset by mêlée and general confusion. In such circumstances the destroyers *Lightning* and *Pakenham* were lost, the former by torpedo from the same German S-boat that had accounted for *Hasty* during the 'Vigorous' operation and the latter being immobilized in the Sicilian Channel and having to be scuttled.

Mines hazarded both sides with impartiality. Echoing the experience of Force 'K' off Tripoli, the Italians lost two destroyers, two torpedo boats and a corvette on a single field. Another victim was the German freighter *Ankara* which, having borne a charmed life over many crossings, was marked by the British. The Narrows became a graveyard for many of the Italians' remaining ships of useful size but, inevitably, these were joined by valuable Allied vessels. Notable among these was the 19,000-ton *Windsor Castle*. With 2,000 troops aboard, she was hit by a single aerial torpedo, succumbing slowly and on an even keel, so that all aboard could be taken off, mostly dry-shod.

The average cargo landed for the Axis army wilted from 64,000 tons monthly to 43,000 tons in March 1943 and only 29,000 tons in April. Loss rates soared to over 41 per cent. March and April alone saw the loss of 69 Axis ships, grossing nearly 128,000 tons. This total did not include the many vessels of less than 500 tons—coasters, ferries, fishing and sailing craft. In six months to early May 1943, over 67,000 troops sailed for North Africa, mostly by destroyer. Over 5,000 perished en route, and the remainder were soon effectively marooned.

To stem the haemorrhage Hitler sent Admiral Dönitz to Rome with powers to act decisively. This resulted in the overdue creation of joint Italo-German staffs in *Comando Supremo*. Admiral Weichold, the senior German naval representative in Rome, was branded too 'pro-Italian' and replaced by Vice-Admiral Ruge, who had much experience in running convoys in the disputed waters of the Eastern Baltic. Weichold had made many contributions, and if his advice regarding the need to take Malta had been heeded, the war in the Mediterranean would have developed very differently.

During the same two months of March and April, some 21,000 Axis troops were flown across to North Africa. Allied fighters abounded and, on occasion, overwhelmed the escort. Vulnerable Ju 52s and lumbering Me 323s went down in dozens, and even the prospect of taking such a flight must have been terrifying.

It remains unbelievable that both Axis powers persisted in pouring resources into what was obviously a lost cause. Mussolini was apprehensive that a war-weary Italy would seize upon the loss of North Africa as a pretext for his overthrow. Hitler, however, retained few scruples about saving the face of his increasingly reluctant ally, yet still considered sacrifice worthwhile.

Early April 1943 saw the Eighth Army ranged against the Wadi Akarit position, the last barrier to a direct run across the coastal plain, virtually all the way to Tunis, 180 miles distant. Only over the four miles from the coast was the wadi itself a major obstacle. For most of its eighteen-mile length, the line relied on a near-continuous 450ft-high ridge, which offered little scope for an armoured breakthrough. Between the ridge and wadi section, however, there was a stretch where two isolated djebels were interspersed with gaps. These were spanned by anti-tank ditches which, in turn, were backed by minefields and covering artillery, whose spotters were sited several hundred yards above. Although the position lacked depth, it was formidable enough, and it had always been favoured by Rommel for a firm stand.

The high ground flanking the gaps was the key to any successful attack, and during the night of 5/6 April the 4th Indian Division, in company with the Sussex, moved silently up the western djebel. They were specialists in this type of assault, but the defending Italians resisted strongly. Only after fierce, hand-to-hand combat (during which a Victoria Cross was earned) was the height taken. By 0830 the djebel was in friendly hands, enabling the western end of the anti-tank ditch, immediately below, to be secured by the Essex. The next phase involved an assault on the djebel on the opposite side of the gap. This was undertaken by the Camerons and Seaforths, following a massive barrage that accounted for a large proportion of the 82,000 shells fired during the Wadi Akarit operation. As the Scots toiled above, the 50th and 51st Divisions broke through the gap and secured it.

So far all had gone according to plan, but an exploitation by corps-sized forces, which were to pass through, wheel and take the remainder of the line from the rear, was inexplicably delayed. As a consequence, the Scots had to spend a further desperate day on the bare ridges above, earning two more Victoria Crosses, while the Germans had time to commit their reserves. Despite massive and continuous attentions from close ground-support aircraft, 40 tanks of the 15th Panzer Division, supported by 88mm guns, arrived to dispute the breach. Entirely in line with Montgomery's philosophy of caution, there was further delay until sufficient artillery had been moved up for a major push on the morning of the 7th. Surprised by their success at halting British progress yet all too aware of the size of the tiger whose tail they were grasping, the Germans persuaded General Messe that the remaining positions would be indefensible once attacked.

By the following morning, therefore, there was no longer a battle to fight but, while Wadi Akarit had been decisively won, Messe had again escaped with the bulk of his army. Nonetheless, 95 per cent of the 5,000 prisoners taken were Italian. The task had probably been lightened by the Americans' successful sidelining of the other two Panzer Divisions, the 10th and 21st. Sealing a joint effort, American and British patrols made contact south of Maknassy late on the 7th. Five months from 'Torch', both Allied armies could now advance shoulder to shoulder. Psychologically, it was an important boost.

With the enemy streaming north along the coastal plain, Alexander attempted an operation to cut them off. This involved pushing an

Anglo-American corps through the narrow Fondouk Gap in the Eastern Dorsale, thence advancing to Kairouan and the sea at Sousse. Difficulty was experienced during the opening phase in the night of 7/8 April in securing the high ground that dominated the gap. As infantry could not take the heights, enemy anti-tank guns and artillery sited on the slopes were able to prevent a whole armoured division from passing.

Aware that Messe was again about to slip the net, Alexander demanded an all-out effort at Fondouk, but it was the afternoon of the 9th before a Guards Brigade could seize the critical djebel that allowed the infantry below to advance and tackle the minefields and their covering gun positions. The follow-through towards Kairouan was thus delayed until the 10th, at which point the Eighth Army had advanced northwards as far as Sfax. Concentrated air support was still a hostage to poor weather, and by the time that Kairouan was taken on 11 April, Messe was safely behind the Enfidaville Line. This system ran in a 100-mile curve to meet the sea again near Bizerta.

Whether a final blow in Tunisia should be cast by the First or Eighth Army appears to have been decided by General Eisenhower himself. Writing to Alexander on 23 March and subsequently, he urged that the thrust be made in the north. Patton's more experienced units should be transferred there 'so as to serve the needs of American morale'. Alexander concurred, drafting the necessary orders to Anderson on 10 April.

Montgomery's request for a further division was refused, the General being informed that the Eighth Army would now adopt a subsidiary role. Worse, one of its existing armoured divisions was to be taken for service further north. Understandably, Montgomery was not pleased, but he later claimed that it was he that suggested to Alexander that the First Army take precedence. His reason was that, while he still faced the Enfidaville defences and further high ground, the quickest way to the capital was via Medjez-el-Bab and Massicault, a route well suited to an armoured thrust.

Alexander's instructions to Montgomery were to pressure the Enfidaville Line sufficiently to keep the enemy's reserves committed; going one better, the Eighth Army commander assaulted the line on 19 and 20 April. If successful he could have advanced to Hammamet and thence across the base of the Cape Bon peninsula, preventing any Bataan-style defence of it by the Axis. Successful, however, he was not. The 50th Division was used to pressure the seaward end of the line while the Indians were again tasked with infiltrating and securing the heights further inland, prior to an outflanking move being staged by the New Zealanders. The Indians stormed and held the first djebel, but it was only the first height of a chain that ran for twelve miles. To seize them all was clearly beyond their resources. Below, during the night of 19/20 April, the New Zealanders fought their way into the key settlement of Takrouna, but at the cost of such a ferocious casualty rate that they could neither advance further nor retreat. For the moment, the order was 'Hold on'.

General Alexander issued the orders for Operation 'Vulcan' on 16 April. This would be the final push, involving five separate thrusts, spaced the length of the Axis perimeter. Both armies, the First and the Eighth, were to be fully committed. They were to be supported by over 3,200 Allied aircraft (which, compared with the 370 that Air Marshal Longmore could deploy in 1940, indicated how far the balance had shifted). Twenty divisions (300,000 men and 1,400 tanks) would squeeze the enemy like pressure applied to a sealed vessel, seeking the weak point that could be exploited for its collapse.

Despite the might of the deployed forces, 'Vulcan' failed, defeated by well-organized resistance in a terrain ideally suited to it. Every djebel, every rock pile, was a natural defensive position. Hard-won locations had often to be abandoned again as the defenders could quite simply walk around them and re-form their line in their rear. 'Vulcan' degenerated rapidly into a grim, slugging match, where success was measured in hundreds of yards. As an exercise it was useful primarily in further depleting the defenders' resources. By 25 April all had again come to a halt.

No ships, other than small craft, reached Bizerta or Tunis after 20 April. Relying now almost totally on air supply, the Axis forces fought on, Kesselring's reason being that the considerable Allied forces thus committed could not be deployed elsewhere. This was of course true—but so was the contrary, and, as the Allies enjoyed the greater overall resources, they would likely be the net beneficiaries. A further justification was the effect on Allied shipping, at a time when the Battle of the Atlantic was reaching its climax. Possession by Axis forces of both shores to the Central Narrows effectively closed the Mediterranean to through traffic. All supplies for the Eighth Army still, therefore, needed to be brought around the Cape, a return trip that occupied the services of each ship involved for several months. As Great Britain supplied most of the mercantile tonnage involved in North African waters, she had suffered a considerable temporary reduction in essential imports, so that strategic stockpiles were known to have been reduced.

Finally, the protracted resistance engendered growing feelings of frustration in the Allied camp: the battle for Tunisia had already gone on far too long. Indeed, the strategic timetable for the Mediterranean demanded an invasion of Sicily by July 1943. A project of this scale could not easily be delayed.

'Ultra' information at this time was maddeningly uninformative. Little was known except for the fact that reinforcements were still being flown in. For some time it had been appreciated that there were now in North

Africa many more trained tank crews than there were tanks for them to man. It was expected by the Allies that these would be given priority in evacuation, but this useful pointer was never available, it being deemed by the Axis High Command that such a withdrawal would adversely affect the morale of those remaining.

Montgomery was ill at this time, but by now he well appreciated that the quickest route to Tunis did not lay through the Enfidaville defences. He requested Alexander to come and discuss the way ahead, and on 30 April the two men agreed that the First Army could be beefed up by some of the Eighth's most experienced formations. These, the 7th Armoured and 4th Indian Infantry Divisions, together with the 201st Guards Brigade, were transferred complete with Montgomery's most highly rated Corps commander, Lt-Gen Horrocks. The rump of the Eighth Army was taken over by Lt-Gen Freyberg, tasked with keeping up the pressure sufficiently to deter the enemy from detaching any units to assist in the defence of Tunis.

Alexander then agreed the final plan (Operation 'Strike') with General Anderson. Horrocks was to lead an advance directly along the already identified axis of Medjez-el-Bab and Massicault. Planned to open on 6 May, it called for the seizure of the high ground and river crossings to the north. The main infantry attack would then thrust through the centre, forming a corridor through which two armoured divisions would pass, heading straight for the capital just 30 miles distant.

Under continuous air cover, the transfers of Eighth Army formations was accomplished within 72 hours. Von Arnim's radio intelligence detected this shift in balance but, though he endeavoured to move as much armour as possible to counter it, shortages of fuel and spares saw only 60 of his tanks transferred. These, together with carefully sited 88s, were concentrated near Massicault.

Even before 'Strike' commenced, Allied spirits were given a fillip when, on 1 May, American pressure in the north caused the Axis line to be pulled back to the east of Mateur. From here, Bizerta was barely 15 miles away and Tunis 25. The defence now had little depth.

Despite the unmistakable signs of Allied activity around Megrez, there was little reaction from the debilitated defence, and, as darkness fell on 5 May, every bomber capable of night bombing hit the enemy rear. At 0300 on the 6th the infantry moved out, unheralded by the usual preliminary bombardment; instead, 650 guns had been amassed, calibrated on to every known enemy forward position and supplied with a staggering 350 rounds per barrel. Laying a creeping barrage five times as intense as the well-remembered shoot that preceded Alamein, these shocked the defenders long enough to allow a virtual walkover. There was little opposition and there were few casualties.

By 0730 the armour was rolling, and two hours later it was passing through the planned secure corridor. Only the narrow front limited the speed of progress. This was relentless, but then, at 1700, and with a retreating opponent reeling ahead, everything came to a halt for the night. Officially it was in order to avoid running too far ahead of supplies, but it demonstrated the usual British failure of refusing to learn from past experience. It also flew in the face of General Alexander's explicit instructions: 'Every effort must be made to pass the two armoured divisions through on the same day . . . so that the enemy is not allowed time to build up a strong anti-tank screen . . . The mopping-up . . . must come later'. Fortunately, the weight of bombardment laid on von Arnim's men so disrupted communications that their general knew little of what was happening. Believing and, indeed, reporting that the bulk of the 15th Panzer Division had been destroyed, he failed to organize the smart counter-attack that would have punished the British dalliance.

From daylight on 7 May it was the turn of the air forces which, in fair weather and with no opposition, pounded at just 25 square miles of concentrated Axis strength. Following a final delay from a determined road block at St Cyprien, the British leading elements entered Tunis during the afternoon, greeted by the greater part of the population and faced by only a few isolated pockets of resistance. To their left, the Americans entered Bizerta and, moving on, met with the British armour. Other forces sealed off the base of the Cape Bon peninsula by 10 May and organized resistance was virtually at an end.

On the American front, the capture of General von Vaerst and his staff led to the surrender of his army. Both von Arnim and Messe still commanded substantial forces, but these, with the sea and the Eighth Army at their backs, were being pushed from the west, north-west and north by the French, Indians and British. As Axis forces were divided, and divided again, resistance became scrappy, and by the 12th the destruction of equipment had commenced. A few minutes after midnight on 12/13 May came the final operational signal from the Axis military forces in North Africa: 'Ammunition shot off. Arms and equipment destroyed. In accordance with orders received DAK has fought itself to a condition where it can fight no more . . .' In the early afternoon of 13 May General Alexander was able to signal to the Prime Minister: 'Sir, it is my duty to report that the Tunisian campaign is over. All enemy resistance has ceased. We are masters of the North African shores.'

There had been a remote prospect of an Axis 'Dunkirk', although circumstances were markedly different. The Narrows here were of the order of 100 miles in width and were dominated totally by Allied ships and aircraft. From 8 May, as soon as the capture of forward airfields permitted standing air cover to be provided, Admiral Cunningham had run day and night patrols by all available destroyers. Termed Operation 'Retribution', doubtless from memories of Greece and Crete, these activities were better known to their participants as the 'Kelibia Regatta'. In accordance with Cunningham's signal 'Sink, burn and destroy. Let nothing pass', his warships intercepted all that moved.

There was little enough of this. About 1,000 Axis troops were captured at sea, heading for Sicily in a variety of makeshift craft, but it was all an anti-climax. Churchill states that '653 are known to have escaped'—an extraordinarily precise figure at a time when imprecision was rife. Early accounts speak of anything between 240,000 and 275,000 Axis prisoners being taken. Alexander quoted 'over 150,000' to Churchill, this figure probably being based on current intelligence estimates. Liddell Hart quotes a report from Army Group Africa to Rome on 2 May that its ration strength varied between 170,000 and 180,000.

While the exact figure is academic, it represented some of the best of the enemy's fighting strength—fit, well-nourished, battle-hardened and, as the Official History comments, with morale unimpaired. These men, and the equipment lost with them, would have faced the Allies in the next phase of the struggle. The recapture of North Africa was, then, a double success—an Axis Army Group removed from the Order of Battle and a territory regained. The next action would be fought on European soil, marking the beginning of the end of the suffering of a continent which had suffered enough.

Select Bibliography

Ando, E., and Bagnasco, E., *Navi e Marinai Italiani nella Seconda Guerra Mondiale*, Albertelli (Parma, 1981).

Attard, Joseph, *The Battle of Malta*, William Kimber (London, 1980).

Auphan, Rear-Admiral Paul, and Mordal, Jacques, *The French Navy in World War II*, US Naval Institute (Annapolis, 1959).

Badoglio, Marshal Pietro, *Italy in the Second World War*, Oxford University Press (London, 1948).

Barnett, Corelli, *The Desert Generals*, William Kimber (London, 1960).

Bekker, Cajus, *The Luftwaffe War Diaries*, Macdonald (London, 1967).

Bennett, Geoffrey, *Cowan's War*, Collins (London, 1964).

Bitzes, John G., *Greece in World War Two to April 1941*, Sunflower University Press, (Yuma, 1989).

Borghese, Count Valerio, *Sea Devils*, Regnery (Chicago, 1954).

Bragadin, Cdr Marc A., *The Italian Navy in World War II*, US Naval Institute (Annapolis, 1957).

Butler, J. R. M., and Gwyer, J. M. A., *Grand Strategy*, HMSO (London, 1957–64).

Carver, Michael, *Tobruk*, Batsford (London, 1964).

Churchill, Sir Winston, *The Second World War*, Cassell (London, 1948).

Cocchia, Admiral Aldo, *The Hunters and the Hunted*, US Naval Institute (Annapolis, 1958).

Collins, Maj-Gen R. J., *Lord Wavell (1883–1941)*, Hodder & Stoughton (London, 1947).

Connell, J., *Wavell*, Cassell (London, 1964).

Cunningham, Admiral of the Fleet Andrew B., *A Sailor's Odyssey*, Hutchinson (London, 1951).

De Belot, Rear-Admiral Raymond, *The Struggle for the Mediterranean 1939–1945*, Princeton University Press (Princeton, 1951).

De Guingand, Frederick, *Operation Victory*, Hodder & Stoughton (London, 1964).

Department of State, *Documents on German Foreign Policy 1918–1954*, US Government Printing Office (Washington, 1949–64).

Dönitz, Admiral Karl, *Memoirs*, Weidenfeld & Nicolson (London, 1959).

Elliott, Peter, *Allied Escort Ships of World War II*, Macdonald & Janes (London, 1977).

Fraccaroli, Aldo, *Italian Warships of World War II*, Ian Allan (London, 1968).

Friedman, Norman, *British Carrier Aviation*, Conway Maritime Press (London, 1988).

Giorgerini, G., and Nani, A., *Gli Incrociatori Italiani 1861–1964*, Ufficio Storico della Marina Militare.

Halpern, Paul G., *The Naval War in the Mediterranean 1914–1918*, Allen & Unwin (London, 1987).

Hezlet, Vice-Admiral Sir Arthur, *Aircraft and Sea Power*, Peter Davies (London, 1970).

————, *The Electron and Sea Power*, Peter Davies (London, 1975).

Hinsley, F. H., *British Intelligence in the Second World War*, HMSO (London, 1981).

Hitler, Adolf, *Hitler's Table Talk*, Weidenfeld & Nicolson (London, 1953).

Hodgkinson, Lt-Cdr Hugh, *Before the Tide Turned*, Harrap (London, 1944).

Hyde, Harlow A., *Scraps of Paper: The Disarmament Treaties between the World Wars*, Media Publishing (Lincoln, Nebraska, 1988).

Jackson, Gen W. G. F., *The North African Campaign*, Batsford (London, 1975).

Keitel, Field Marshal Wilhelm, *Memoirs*, William Kimber (London, 1965).

Kesselring, Field Marshal Albrecht, *Memoirs*, Greenhill (London, 1988).

King, Fleet Admiral Ernest J., and Whitehill, Cdr W., *Fleet Admiral King: A Naval Record*, Eyre & Spottiswoode (London, 1953).

Laird Clowes, Sir William, *et al*, *The Royal Navy: A History*, Sampson Low, Marston & Co (London, 1903).

Lewin, Ronald, *Ultra Goes to War*, Hutchinson (London, 1978).

Liddell Hart, Sir Basil H., *History of the Second World War*, Cassell (London, 1970).

Lloyd, Air Marshal Sir Hugh, *Brief to Attack*.

Lutton, Wayne C., *Malta and the Mediterranean*, University Microfilms International.

Mac Smith, D., *Mussolini*, Weidenfeld & Nicolson (London, 1981).

Marder, Arthur J., *From the Dardanelles to Oran*, Oxford University Press (London, 1974).

————, *From the Dreadnought to Scapa Flow*, Oxford University Press (London, 1961–70).

Montgomery, Field Marshal Viscount, *Memoirs*, Odhams (London, 1958).

Moorehead, Alan, *African Triology*, Hamish Hamilton (London, 1944).

Morison, Samuel Eliot, *History of US Naval Operations in World War II*, Vol II, Oxford University Press (London, 1947).

Muggeridge (ed.), *Ciano's Diary 1939–1943*, Heinemann (London, 1947).

Murray, Marischal, *Union-Castle Chronicle 1853–1953*, Longmans (London, 1953).

Ollard, Richard, *Fisher and Cunningham*, Constable (London, 1991).

Playfair, Maj-Gen I. S. O., *et al*, *The Mediterranean and the Middle East*, HMSO (London, 1960).

Raeder, Grand Admiral Erich, *Struggle for the Sea*, William Kimber (London, 1959).

Richard, D., and Saunders, H. St G., *The Royal Air Force 1939–1945*, HMSO (London, 1953).

Rohwer, J., and Hummelchen, G., *Chronology of the War at Sea*, Ian Allan (London, 1972).

Rommel, Field Marshal Erwin, *The Rommel Papers*, Collins (London, 1953).

Roskill, Capt Stephen W., *Naval Policy between the Wars*, Collins (London, 1968).

————, *The War at Sea*, HMSO (London, 1954–61).

Ruge, Vice-Admiral Friedrich, *Sea Warfare 1939–1945: A German Viewpoint*, Cassell (London, 1957).

Simpson, Rear-Admiral G. W. G., *Periscope View*, Macmillan (London, 1972).

Taylor, A. J. P., *The Origins of the Second World War*, Hamish Hamilton (London, 1961).

Vian, Admiral of the Fleet Sir Philip, *Action This Day*, Muller (London, 1960).

Von Mellenthin, Maj-Gen F. W., *Panzer Battles 1939–45*, Cassell (London, 1955).

Winton, John, *Ultra at Sea*, Leo Cooper (London, 1988).

Young, Desmond, *Rommel*, Collins (London, 1950).

Index

Nullo (Italian destroyer), 55

'O' class submarines (Dutch), 92
Oceania (Italian liner), 99
'Ochsenkopf', Operation, 197
O'Connor, General Sir Richard, 57, 60–1, 66
Odin, HMS, 35
Ohio (US tanker), 150–2
Oil supplies, 17, 22, 48–9, 56, 74, 90, 101, 148,
    171, 183, 191, 197
OKH (German Army Supreme Command), 66
OKM (German Naval Supreme Command), 18
OKW (Supreme Command of German Armed
    Forces), 197
Olterra (Italian tanker), 154
Olympus, HMS, 122
Operational Intelligence Centre (OIC), 16
Oran, 170, 174–6
Orari (British freighter), 133, 149
Orion, HMS, 51, 76, 88
Orpheus, HMS, 35
Ostro (Italian destroyer), 34, 39
Otranto, Strait of, 51

P36, HMS, 118, 122
'Pact of Steel', 16, 17
Pakenham, HMS, 205
Pampas (British freighter), 119–20
Pandora, HMS, 122
Pantellaria Island, 41, 49, 73, 97, 98, 132, 151
Panzer III tank, 125, 157
Panzer IV tank, 195
Panzer VI tank, 160, 186, 195, 197
Park, Air Vice-Marshal K. R., 136, 147
Parracombe (British freighter), 71
Parramatta, HMAS, 68
Parthian, HMS, 90
Partridge, HMS, 132–3, 185
Patton, General George S., 176, 201, 203, 208
'Pedestal', Operation, 147–53
Pegaso (Italian torpedo boat), 122
Peloponnesus, 81–2
Penelope, HMS, 102, 106, 117, 122
Penn, HMS, 152
Pericles (Norwegian tanker), 75
Perim Island, 34–5
'Perpetual', Operation, 104
Perseo (Italian torpedo boat), 192
Persia, 90
Pétain, Marshal Henri, 171, 178
Phoebe, HMS, 89
Phoenix, HMS, 36
Pilo (Italian torpedo boat), 34
Piraeus, 80, 85
Ploesti, 48, 56
Pola (Italian cruiser), 59, 77
Poland, Capt A. L., 123–4
Porcupine, HMS, 185
Port Chalmers (British freighter), 151
'Portcullis', Operation, 182
Port Lyautey, 176

Porto Raphti, 81
Port Said, 35
Pound, Admiral of the Fleet Sir Dudley, 39, 45
Preussen (German freighter), 98
Pridham-Wippell, Admiral H. D., 51, 76, 120
Prince of Wales, HMS, 100
Prinz Eugen (German cruiiser), 116
Procida (Italian tanker), 103
Provence (French battleship), 25, 31
Punta Stilo, see Calabria

Qattara Depression, 137, 140, 164
Queen Elizabeth, HMS, 21, 67, 105–7, 124
Quentin, HMS, 185

R-boats, 100
'R' class battleships, 25, 37
Raeder, Grand Admiral Erich, 33, 61, 95, 98,
    100, 137, 194
Ramillies, HMS, 49, 52
Ramsey, Admiral Sir Bertram, 170
Rangers, US, 173–4
Rashid Ali, 89
Raw, Capt S. M., 58
Rawlings, Admiral H. B., 84–8, 103
Re 2001, Reggiane, 116, 149
Regolo (Italian cruiser), 182
Regulus, HMS, 58
Renouf, Admiral E. de F., 62–4
Renown, HMS, 53–4
Resolution, HMS, 29
'Retribution', Operation, 212
Reynard, Paul, 27
Riccardi, Admiral Arturo, 57
Richelieu (French battleship), 23, 25, 28, 177,
    183
Ritchie, General N. M., 109, 114, 124–8, 137–8
Roberts, HMS, 183
Rochester Castle (British freighter), 151
Rodney, HMS, 100, 147
Roma (Italian battleship), 23
Romania, 52, 56, 80, 83, 95
Rommel, General Erwin, 62, 65–6, 93, 95, 98,
    99, 107–10, 114, 124, 137–45, 154–60,
    162–9, 179, 187 et seq.
Roosevelt, President Franklin D., 27, 111–13,
    121, 131, 172, 193
'Round-Up', Operation, 140
Royal Sovereign, HMS, 36
Rubino (Italian submarine), 39
Ruck-Keene, Capt P., 136
Ruge, Admiral Friedrich, 206
Russo-German Non-Aggression Pact, 18, 20, 52
Ruweisat Ridge, 141, 143, 156
Rye, HMS, 152

S-boats, 100, 122, 134, 205
Safari, HMS, 182
Safi, 176
Sagittario (Italian torpedo boat), 85
Sagona (Norwegian tanker), 106–7